図解300

明治・日本人の住まいと暮らし
モースが魅せられた美しく豊かな住文化

JAPANESE HOMES AND THEIR SURROUNDINGS
with ILLUSTRATIONS by EDWARD S. MORSE

阿吽社——編集　　紫紅社——発行

JAPANESE HOMES
AND THEIR SURROUNDINGS
with ILLUSTRATIONS
by EDWARD S. MORSE

Originally published by
Ticknor and Company, Boston, in 1886.

Copyright ⓒ 2017 by Aunsha, Kyoto.
All rights reserved.

はじめに

　この本は、明治の初めに来日したアメリカ人博物学者、エドワード・シルヴェスター・モース Edward Sylvester Morse の著書 *"JAPANESE HOMES and Their Surroundings"* (Ticknor and Company, Boston, 1886) のイラスト・図版を抽出して構成しています（原書名を直訳すれば、『日本（人）の住まいとその周囲環境』とでもなるでしょうか）。

　モースは、1877（明治10）年に「お雇い外国人」として東京大学の動物学・生理学教授に就任しました。大森貝塚の発見・発掘にたずさわったことでも、よく知られています。1883（明治16）年までに3度来日、通算3年以上日本に滞在しましたが、この期間モースは大学での進化論講義や大森貝塚にかかわる講演などを行なって、日本学術界に多大なる貢献をしています。一方、東京各地や関東近郊のみならず、日本列島各地を調査旅行し、膨大な量の民具や陶磁器などを収集してアメリカに持ち帰りました。総数は数万点以上ともいわれていますが、その多くはアメリカのピーボディ・エセックス博物館（マサチューセッツ州セイラム）やボストン美術館に収蔵されています。

　モースが持ち帰った民具・民芸品など庶民の生活道具は、現代の日本では見かけられないものが多く、100年以上経った日本に里帰りする展覧会も何度か開かれて多くの来場者を集め、そのときの図録や写真集なども評判をよびました。

　モースは当時まだ珍しかった写真も撮影していますが、多くのスケッチも残していて、学者としての観察眼の鋭さだけでなく、確かな絵心も持っていたことがわかります。この本に掲載した300点以上のイラスト・図版のほとんどは、モースのスケッチをもとにおこされたものと思われますが、その精密さと絵としての完成度の高さから、明治初めの日本を知る貴重な歴史資料であることは、疑いありません。

　この本では日本の家の建て方や外観にも言及されていますが、モースの関心は「日本の住宅」そのものよりも、「日本人の住まい方」「日本人の暮らしぶり」にあったと思われます。そのことは原書名に "house" ではなく "home" の語が使われていることからも、推測できることでしょう。

　明治10年代の日本は、維新政府の推し進める「文明開化」の真っただ中

にあったのですが、まだまだ江戸時代の香りを色濃く残す時代でもありました。モースは当初、西洋とは異なる東洋の文化に、博物学者としての興味をそそられたのでしょうが、徐々にその文化の奥深さに魅かれ、愛情を覚えるようになっていったのでしょう。このイラスト集をながめるだけでも、そのことがよくわかります。

　モースのスケッチには、当時の日本人たちの、現代から見ればけっして裕福ではない住生活が描かれています。しかしその一方で、そこになんとも「ゆたかな暮らしぶり」があることをモースは見てとって、それらを愛しているであろうことも伝わってくるのです。祖父母や曾祖父母・高祖父母たち先人の暮らしぶりを知る手がかりを、異邦人モースがのこしてくれたことに、私たちは感謝しなければならないでしょう。

　明治維新からもうすぐ 150 年の時を数えます。モースが魅せられ愛した「日本の家庭風景」は、昭和 30 年代くらいまでは日本各地に幾分かはのこっていたと思われますが、モースのスケッチをながめて、記憶の底にあるなつかしさを覚えられる人は数少なくなってきたことでしょう。しかしまだ、「初めて見たのに、なぜかなつかしい」と感じていただける若い人も少なからずいるのではないでしょうか。

　通りや庭に出ている人たち（p.19 ～ 33 など）の姿かたちを見るだけでも、人それぞれいろいろな想いがわきあがってくることと思います。そうした「日本的なるものへの郷愁」を、多くの人に感じ取っていただければ、この本の企画・編集にたずさわったものとして喜びにたえません。

２０１７年４月

編　者

追　記
本書のイラスト・図版などは、原著第 1 版から写したが、縮尺は随時変更している。
「図版解説」は原著図版キャプションに本文内容や最新の情報も加味して訳出した。
巻末に、原著の「LIST OF ILLUSTRATIONS 図版リスト」と「GLOSSARY 用語解説」（日本住文化の和英辞書として使用可）を付した。
下記の原著邦訳書を図版解説の訳出などに参考にさせていただきました。
『日本人の住まい』斎藤正二・藤本周一／訳、八坂書房、1979 年。
『日本のすまい・内と外』上田篤・加藤晃規・柳美代子／共訳、鹿島出版会、1979 年。
また、日本に関わるモースの著書として、下記のものがある。
『日本その日その日』全 3 巻、石川欣一／訳、平凡社東洋文庫、1970 年（原著 *"Japan Day By Day"*, 1917）。

明治・日本人の住まいと暮らし ● もくじ

はじめに ……… 3

街と村の風景 〈Fig.1 - 3〉 ……… 8
住まいの建て方 〈Fig.4 - 25〉 ……… 9
大工道具など 〈Fig. 26 - 32〉 ……… 17
都市と郊外の民家 〈Fig. 33 - 59〉 ……… 19
板屋根 など 〈Fig. 60 - 66〉 ……… 34
瓦屋根 など 〈Fig. 67 - 77〉 ……… 35
茅葺き屋根 など 〈Fig. 78 - 95〉 ……… 38
室内・間取り・畳・引戸 など 〈Fig. 96 - 118〉 ……… 43
床の間と違い棚を見せるインテリア 〈Fig. 119 - 129〉 ……… 50
茶 室 〈Fig. 130 - 135〉 ……… 56
蔵のインテリア など 〈Fig. 136 - 142〉 ……… 60
天井・欄間・窓 〈Fig. 143 - 154〉 ……… 63
屛風・衝立・簾・暖簾 など 〈Fig. 155 - 166〉 ……… 66
台所・階段 など 〈Fig. 167 - 179〉 ……… 68
風呂場・洗面所 など 〈Fig. 180 - 192〉 ……… 74
枕・火鉢・たばこ盆 〈Fig. 193 - 204〉 ……… 76
燭台・行灯・神棚 〈Fig. 205 - 216〉 ……… 78
かわや 〈Fig. 217 - 220〉 ……… 80
玄 関 〈Fig. 221 - 225〉 ……… 82
縁 側 〈Fig. 226 - 232〉 ……… 84
雨 戸 〈Fig. 233 - 237〉 ……… 86

手水鉢 〈Fig. 238 - 241〉 ……… *87*

門 〈Fig. 242 - 253〉 ……… *88*

塀・垣 〈Fig. 254 - 262〉 ……… *94*

灯籠 など 〈Fig. 263 - 267〉 ……… *96*

庭の橋 〈Fig. 268 - 270〉 ……… *97*

東屋・窓・路地 〈Fig. 271 - 275〉 ……… *98*

植木鉢・盆栽 など 〈Fig.276 - 282〉 ……… *99*

庭の景色 〈Fig. 283 - 286〉 ……… *101*

井戸・給水 など 〈Fig. 287 - 293〉 ……… *105*

花 〈Fig. 294 - 297〉 ……… *107*

いろいろな物 〈Fig. 298 - 302〉 ……… *108*

その他の家 〈Fig.303 - 307〉 ……… *110*

図版解説 ……… *112*

LIST OF ILLUSTRATIONS （図版リスト） ……… *127*

GLOSSARY （用語解説・和英辞書） ……… *137*

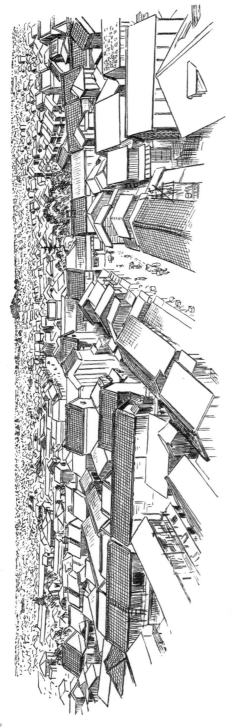

Fig. 1. — A View in Tokio, showing Shops and Houses. (Copied from a Photograph.)

Fig. 2. — A View in Tokio, showing Temples and Gardens. (Copied from a Photograph.)

FIG. 3. — VIEW OF ENOSHIMA. (COPIED FROM A PHOTOGRAPH.)

FIG. 4. — SIDE FRAMING.

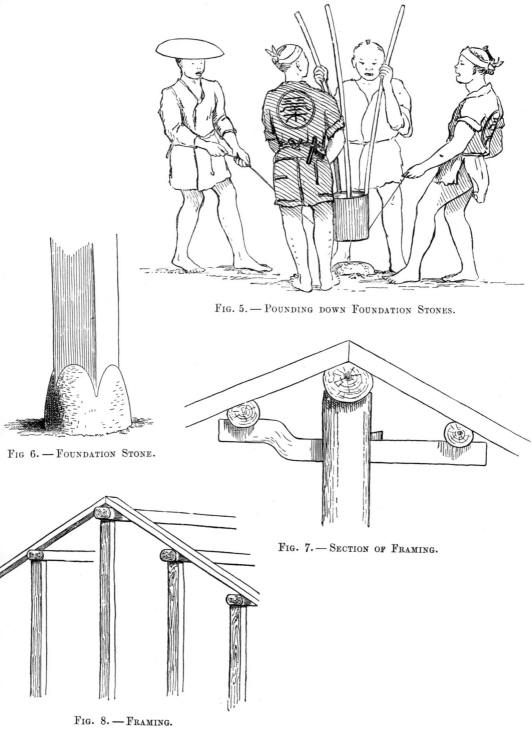

Fig. 5. — Pounding down Foundation Stones.

Fig. 6. — Foundation Stone.

Fig. 7. — Section of Framing.

Fig. 8. — Framing.

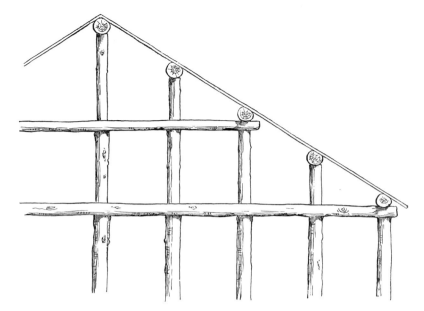

Fig. 9.— End-framing of large Building.

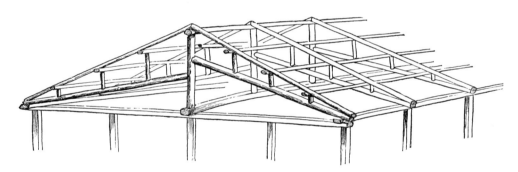

Fig. 10.— Roof-frame of large Building.

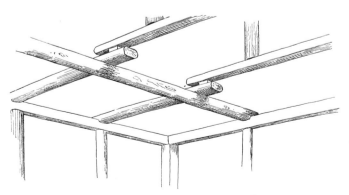

Fig. 11.— Roof-framing of Kura.

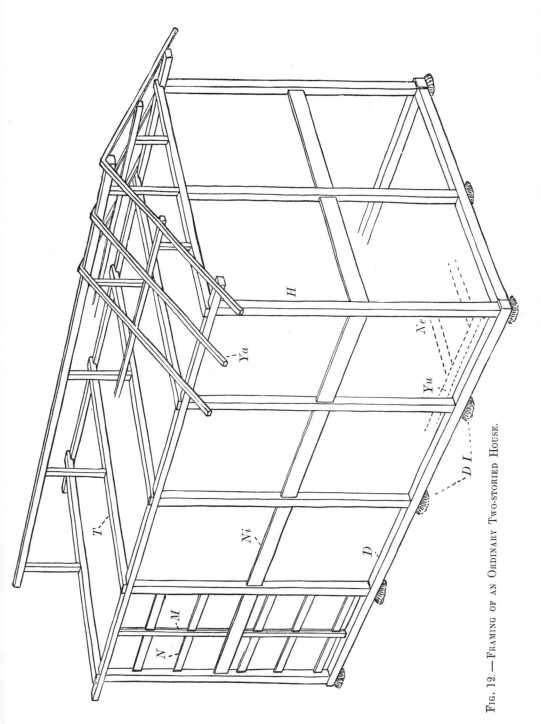

Fig. 12.—Framing of an Ordinary Two-storied House.

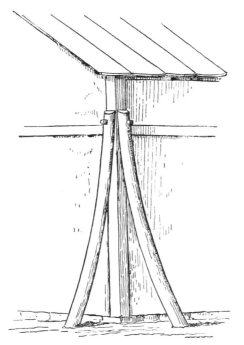

Fig. 13. — Outside Braces.

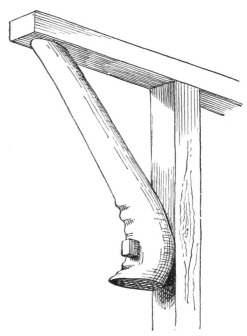

Fig. 14. — Outside Brace.

Fig. 15. — Ornamental Brace.

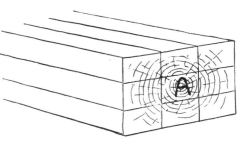

Fig. 16. — Method of Cutting Timber for House-finish.

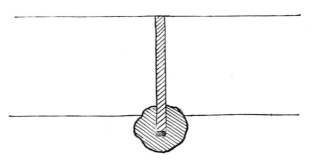

Fig. 17. — Section of Post Grooved for Partition.

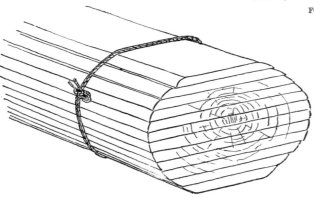

Fig. 18. — Bundle of Boards.

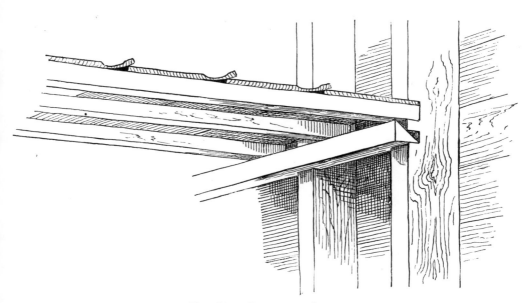

Fig. 19. — Section of Ceiling.

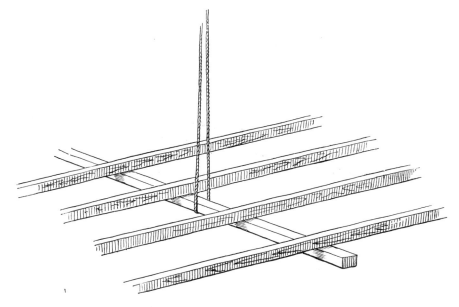

Fig. 20. — Ceiling-rafters supported temporarily.

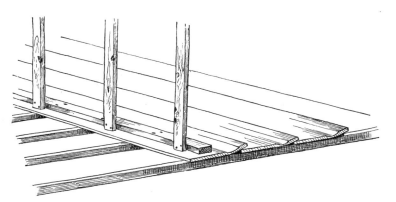

Fig. 21. — Method of Suspending Ceiling as seen from above.

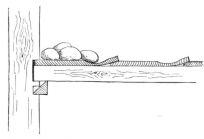

Fig. 22. — Ceiling-board Weighted with Stones.

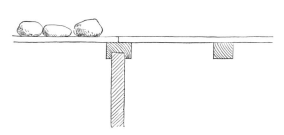

Fig. 23. — Ceiling-board in Closet.

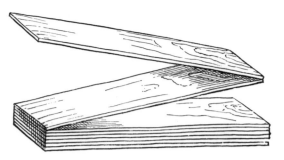

Fig. 24. — Method of removing Boards from Bundle to Preserve Uniformity of Grain.

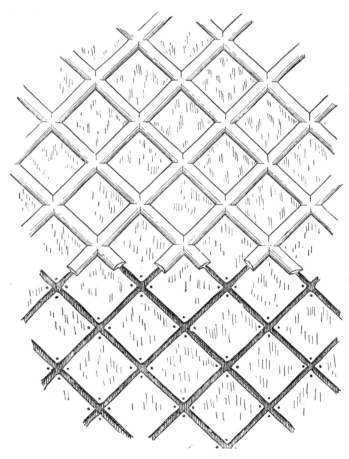

Fig. 25. — Arrangement of Square Tiles on Side of House.

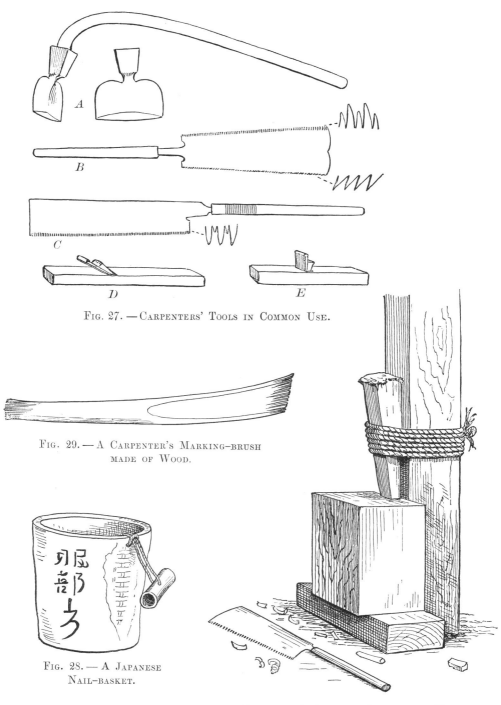

Fig. 27. — Carpenters' Tools in Common Use.

Fig. 29. — A Carpenter's Marking-brush made of Wood.

Fig. 28. — A Japanese Nail-basket.

Fig. 26. — A Japanese Carpenter's Vise.

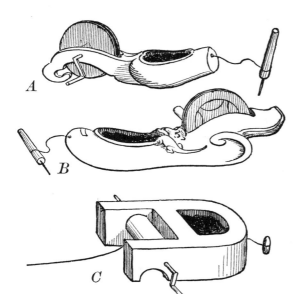

Fig. 30. — The Sumi-tsubo.

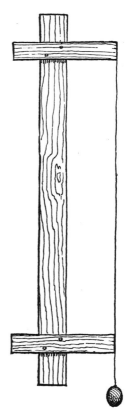

Fig. 31.
The Japanese
Plumb-line.

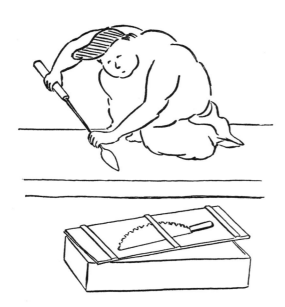

Fig. 32. — Ancient Carpenter. (Copied from an Old Painting.)

Fig. 33. — Street in Kanda Ku, Tokio.

Fig. 34. — Street in Kanda Ku, Tokio.

Fig. 35. — Block of Cheap Tenements in Tokio.

Fig. 36. — Street View of Dwelling in Tokio.

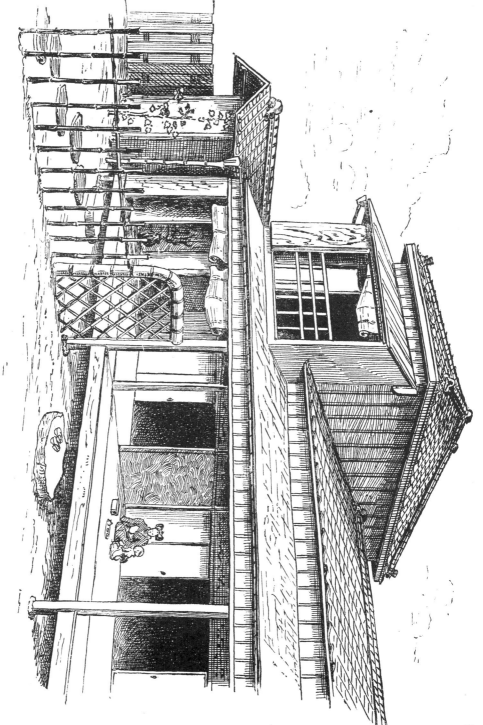

Fig. 37. — View of Dwelling from Garden, in Tokio.

Fig. 38. — Dwelling near Kudan, Tokio.

Fig. 39. — Country Inn in Rikuzen.

Fig. 40. — Country Inn in Rikuzen.

Fig. 41. — House near Mororan, Yezo.

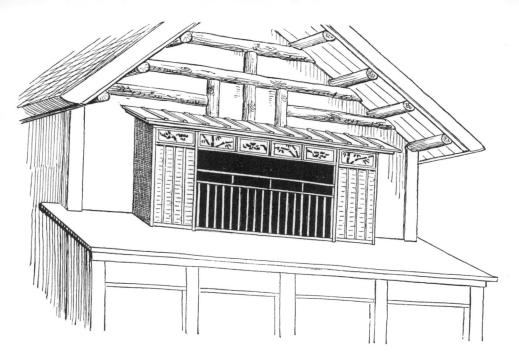

Fig. 42. — Bay-window, Village of Odzuka, Rikuzen.

Fig. 43. — Three-storied House in Rikuchiu.

Fig. 44. — Street in the Suburbs of Morioka.

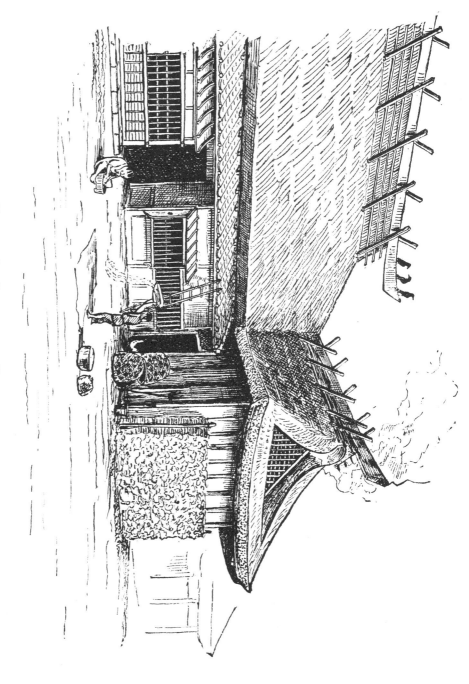

Fig. 45. — Old Farm-house in Kabutoyama.

Fig. 46. — Entrance to Court-yard of Old House in Kioto.

Fig. 47. — Old House in Kioto. Court-yard View.

Fig. 48. — Old House in Kioto. Garden View.

Fig. 49. — House in Tokio.

Fig. 50. — View from Second Story of Dwelling in Imado, Tokio.

Fig. 51. — Old Inn in Mishima, Suruga.

Fig. 52. — Village Street in Nagaike, Yamashiro.

Fig. 53. — Shore of Osumi.

Fig. 54. — Farmers' Houses in Mototarumidsu, Osumi.

Fig. 55. — Fishermen's Huts in Hakodate.

Fig. 56. — Fishermen's Houses at Enoshima.

Fig. 57. — Kura in Tokio.

Fig. 58. — Kura, or Fire-proof Buildings in Tokio.

Fig. 59. — Old House in Hakodate.

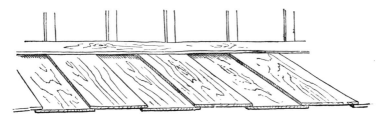

Fig. 60. — Hisashi.

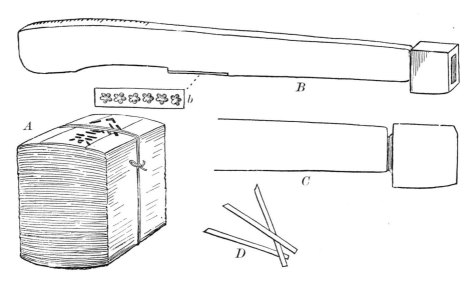

Fig. 61. — Bunch of Shingles, Nails, and Hammer.

Fig. 62. — Shingler's Hand.   Fig. 63. — Bamboo Strips on Shingle-roof.

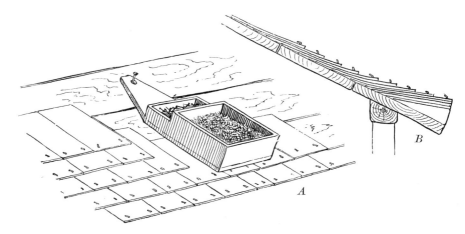

Fig. 64. — Roof with Shingles partly laid.

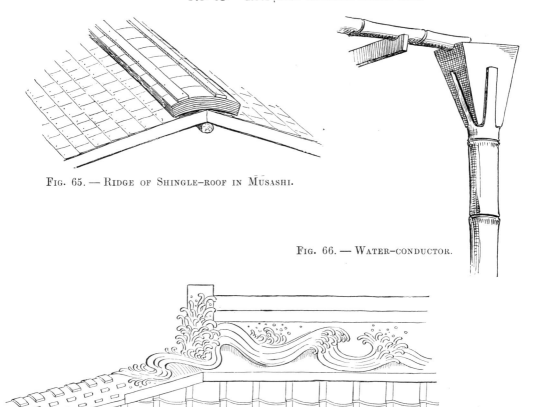

Fig. 65. — Ridge of Shingle-roof in Musashi.

Fig. 66. — Water-conductor.

Fig. 67. — Ridge of Tiled Roof.

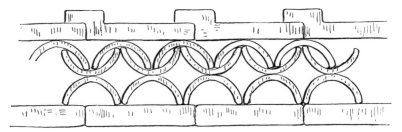

Fig. 68. — Ornamental Coping of Tiles.

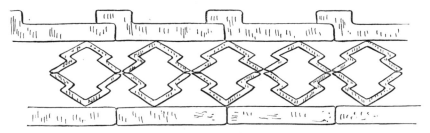

Fig. 69. — Ornamental Coping of Tiles.

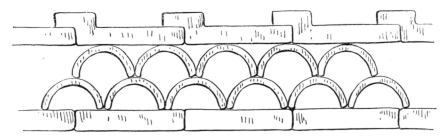

Fig. 70. — Ornamental Coping of Tiles.

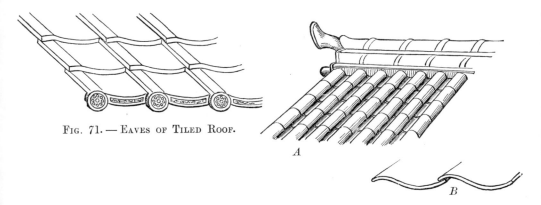

Fig. 71. — Eaves of Tiled Roof.

Fig. 72. — Nagasaki Tiled Roof.

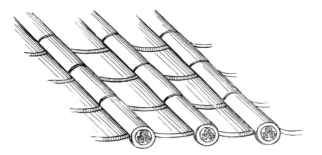

Fig. 73. — Hon-gawara, or True Tile.

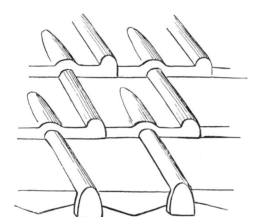

Fig. 74. — Yedo-gawara, or Yedo-tile Eaves.

Fig. 75. — French Tile Eaves

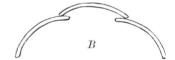

Fig. 76. — Iwami Tile for Ridge.

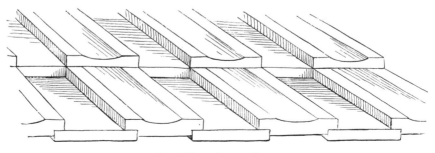

Fig. 77. — Stone Roof.

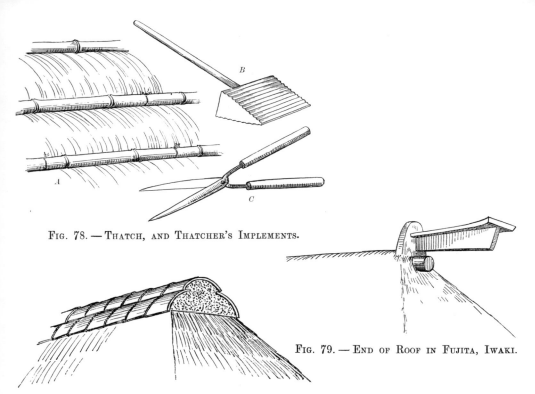

Fig. 78. — Thatch, and Thatcher's Implements.

Fig. 79. — End of Roof in Fujita, Iwaki.

Fig. 80. — Tiled Ridge of Thatched Roof in Iwaki.

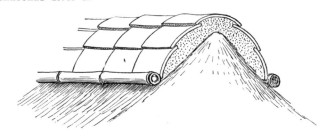

Fig. 81. — Tiled Ridge of Thatched Roof in Musashi.

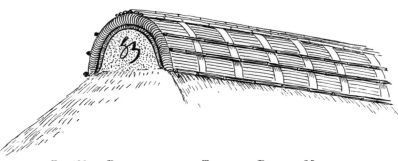

Fig. 82. — Bamboo-ridge of Thatched Roof in Musashi.

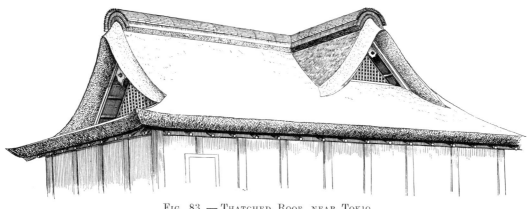

Fig. 83. — Thatched Roof, near Tokio.

Fig. 84. — Thatched Roof, near Tokio.

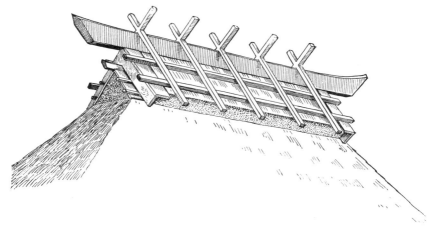

Fig. 85. — Ridge of Thatched Roof at Kabutoyama, Musashi.

Fig. 86. — Crest of Thatched Roof in Omi.

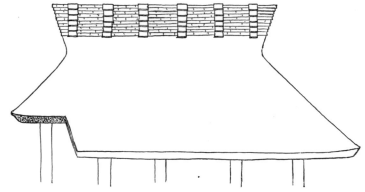

Fig. 87. — Tile and Bamboo Ridge of Thatched Roof, Takatsuki, Setsu.

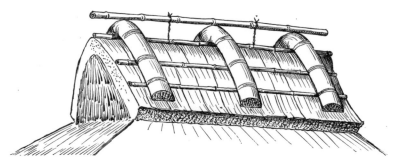

Fig. 88. — Crest of Thatched Roof in Mikawa.

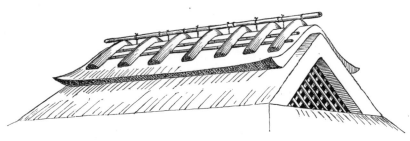

Fig. 89. — Crest of Thatched Roof in Kioto.

Fig. 90. — Crest of Thatched Roof in Mikawa.

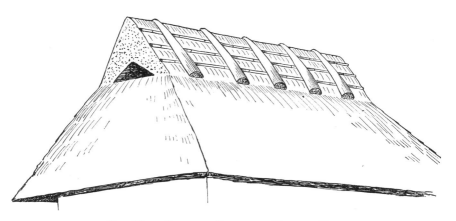

Fig. 91. — Crest of Thatched Roof in Kii.

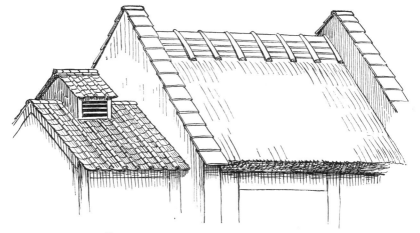

Fig. 92. — Thatched Roof in Yamato.

Fig. 93. — Crest of Thatched Roof in Totomi.

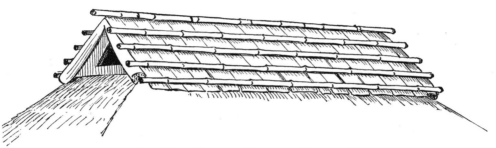

Fig. 94. — Crest of Thatched Roof in Ise.

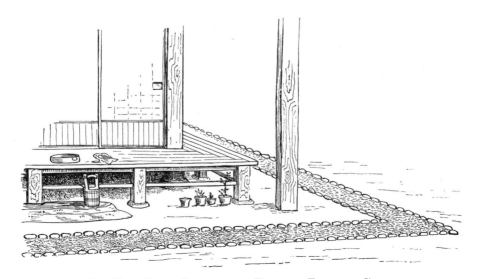

Fig. 95. — Paved Space under Eaves of Thatched Roof.

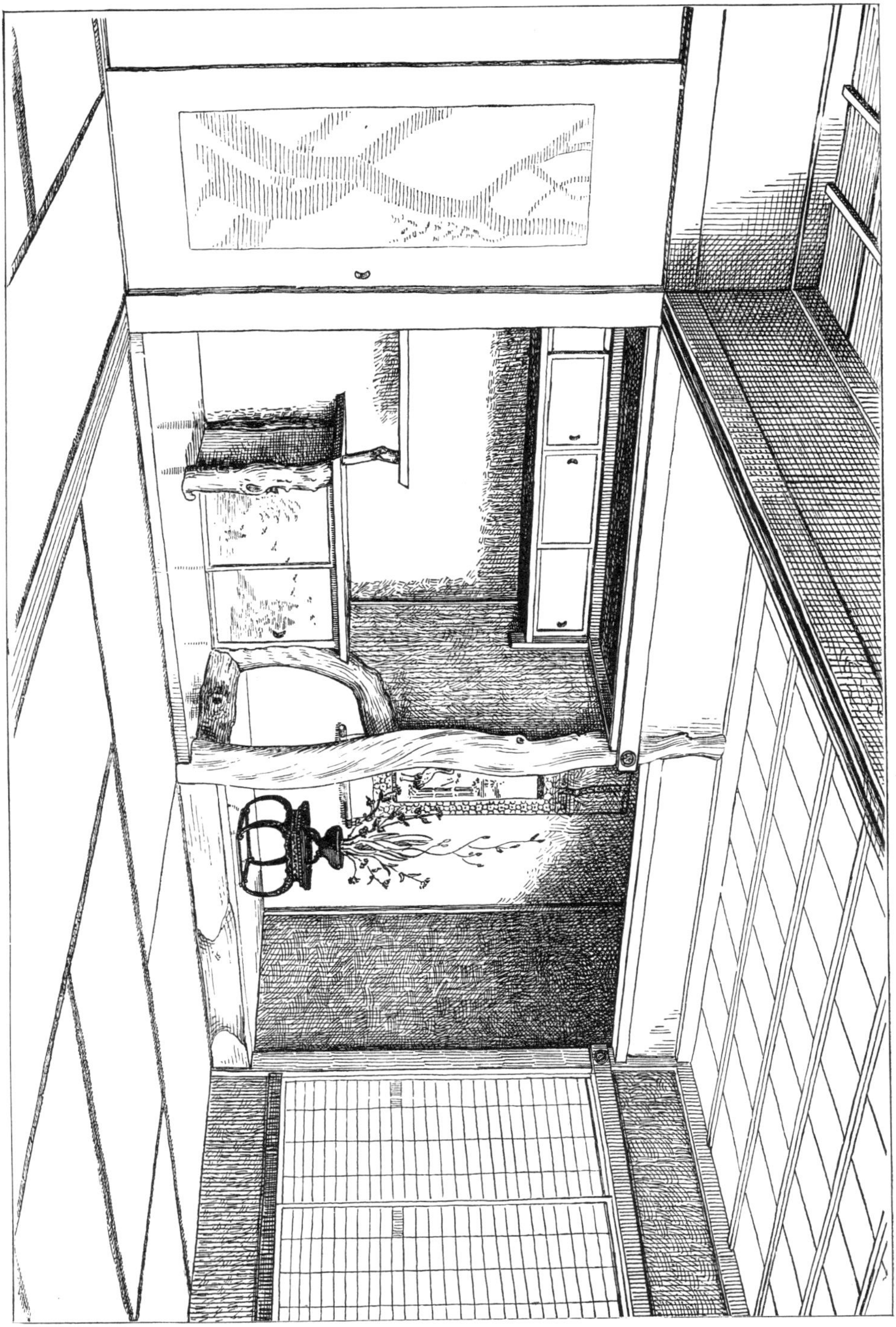

FIG. 96.— GUEST-ROOM IN HACHI-ISHI.

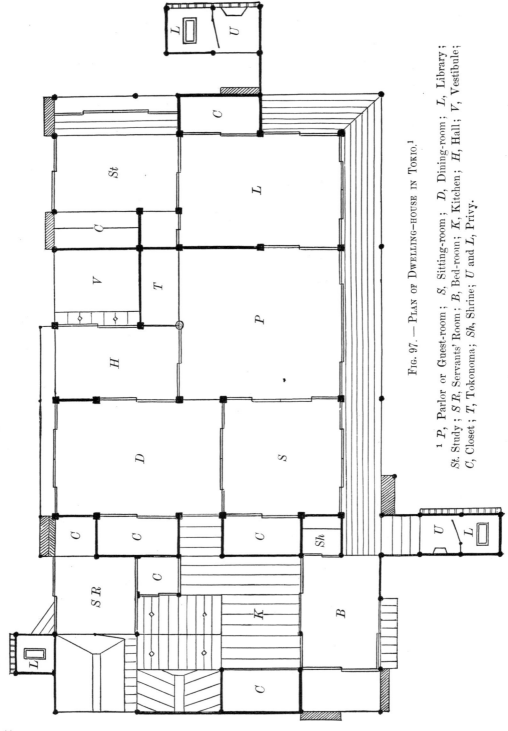

Fig. 97. — Plan of Dwelling-house in Tokio.[1]

[1] *P*, Parlor or Guest-room; *S*, Sitting-room; *D*, Dining-room; *L*, Library; *St*. Study; *S R*, Servants' Room; *B*, Bed-room; *K*, Kitchen; *H*, Hall; *V*, Vestibule; *C*, Closet; *T*, Tokonoma; *Sh*, Shrine; *U* and *L*, Privy.

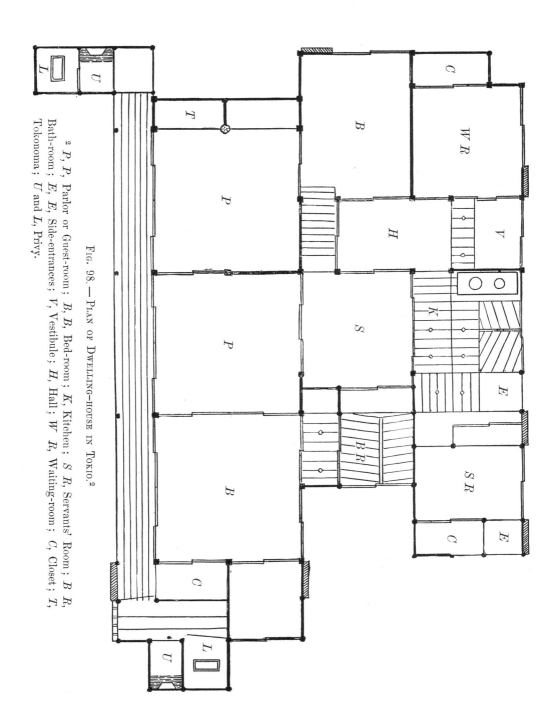

Fig. 98. — Plan of Dwelling-house in Tokio.[2]

[2] P, P, Parlor or Guest-room; B, B, Bed-room; K, Kitchen; $S R$, Servants' Room; $B R$, Bath-room; E, E, Side-entrances; V, Vestibule; H, Hall; $W R$, Waiting-room; C, Closet; T, Tokonoma; U and L, Privy.

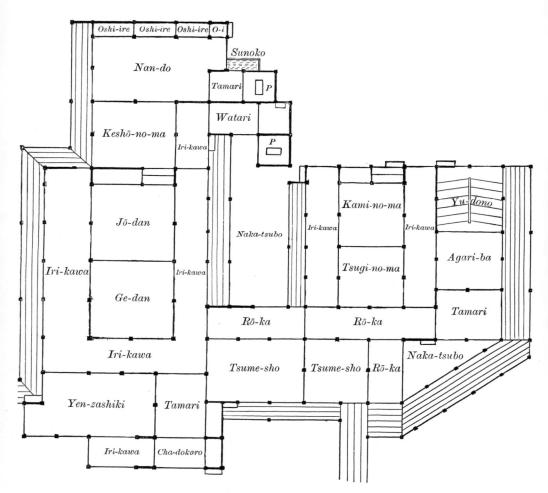

FIG. 99. — PLAN OF A PORTION OF A DAIMIO'S RESIDENCE.[1]

[1] The following is a brief explanation of the names of the rooms given in plan fig. 99: *Agari-ba* (*Agari*, "to go up;" *ba*, "place"), Platform, or place to stand on in coming out of the Bath. *Cha-dokoro*, Tea-place; *Ge-dan*, Lower Step; *Jō-dan*, Upper Step; *Iri-kawa*, Space between verandah and room; *Kami-no-ma*, Upper place or room; *Tsugi-no-ma*, Next place or room; *Keshō-no-ma*, Dressing-room (*Keshō*, — "adorning the face with powder"). *Nan-do*, Store-room; *Naka-tsubo*, Middle space; *Oshi-ire*, Closet (literally, "push," "put in"); *Rō-ka*, Corridor, Covered way; *Tamari*, Ante-chamber; *Tsume-sho*, Waiting-room for servants; *Yu-dono*, Bath-room; *Yen-zashiki*, End parlor; *Watari*, — "to cross over;" *Sunoko*. Bamboo shelf or platform.

Fig. 100. — Mat.

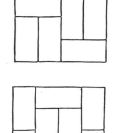

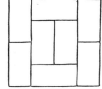

Fig. 102. — Attitude of Woman in Sitting.

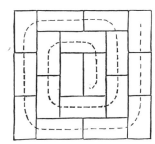

Fig. 101. — Arrangement of Mats in different-sized Rooms.

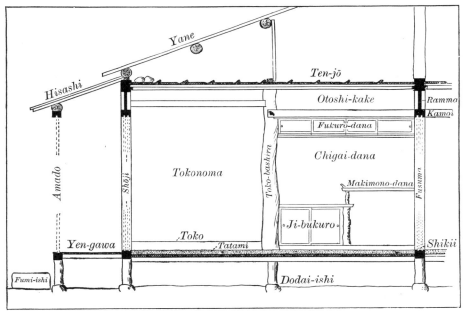

Fig. 103. — Section through Verandah and Guest-room.

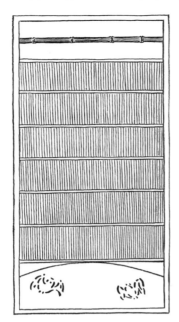

Fig. 104. — Reed-screen.

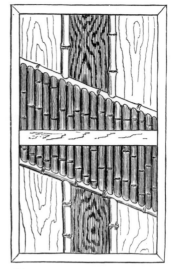

Fig. 105. — Sliding Panel.

Fig. 106. — Hikite.

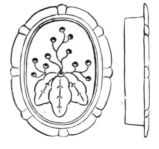

Fig. 107. — Hikite.

Fig. 108. — Hikite.

Fig. 109. — Hikite.

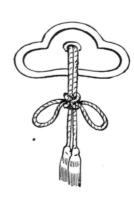

Fig. 110. — Hikite with Cord.

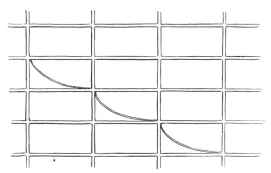

FIG. 111. — STRAIGHTENING SHŌJI FRAME.

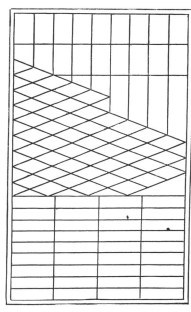

FIG. 112. — SHŌJI WITH ORNAMENTAL FRAME.

FIG. 113. PORTION OF TOKO-BASHIRA.

FIG. 118. — SHELVES CONTRASTED WITH CONVENTIONAL DRAWING OF MIST, OR CLOUDS.

FIGS. 114, 115, 116, AND 117. ORNAMENTAL-HEADED NAILS.

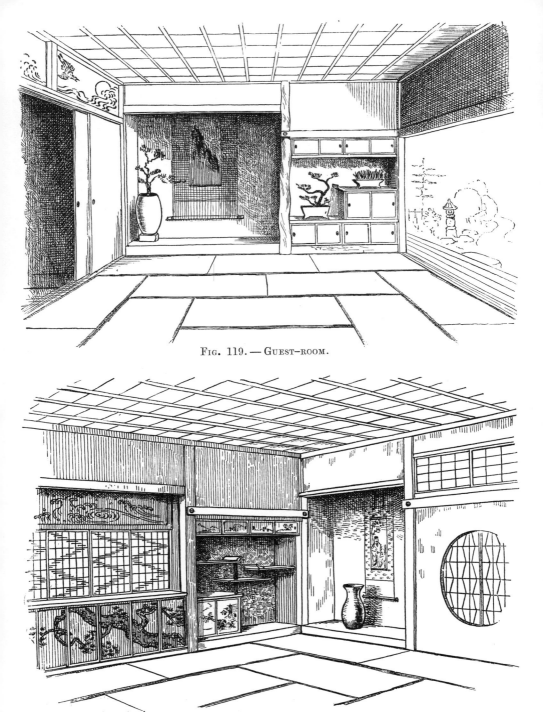

Fig. 119. — Guest-room.

Fig. 120. — Guest-room, with Recesses in Corner.

Fig. 121. — Guest-room showing Circular Window.

Fig. 122. — Guest-room showing Writing-place.

Fig. 123. — Guest-room with wide Tokonoma.

Fig. 124. — Small Guest-room.

Fig. 125. — Guest-room of Dwelling in Tokio.

Fig. 126. — Guest-room in Kiyomidzu, Kioto.

Fig. 127. — Guest-room of Dwelling in Tokio.

Fig. 128. — Guest-room of a Country House.

Fig. 129. — Corner of Guest-room.

Fig. 130. — Tea-room in Nan-en-ji Temple, Kioto.

Fig. 131. — Tea-room in Fujimi Pottery, Nagoya.

Fig. 132. — Tea-room in Miyajima.

Fig. 133. — Kitchen for Tea-utensils.

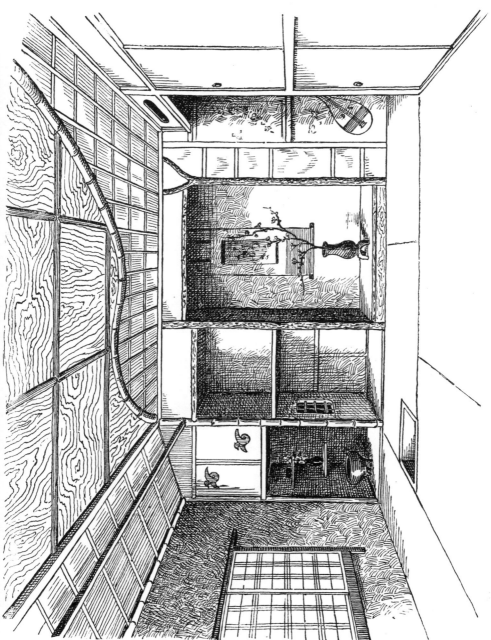

Fig. 134. — Tea-room in Imado, Tokio.

Fig. 135. — Corner of Tea-room shown in Fig. 134.

Fig. 136. — Room in Second Story of Old Building in Kawagoye, Musashi.

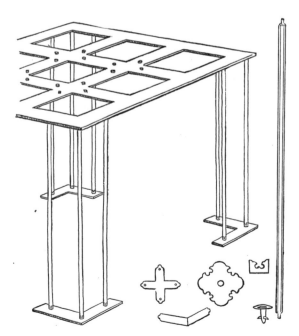

Fig. 138. — Framework for Draping Room in Kura.

Fig. 137. — Room in Kura fitted up as a Library, Tokio.

Fig. 140. — Doorway of an old Kura in Kioto.

Fig. 139. — Space between Dwelling and Kura, roofed over and utilized as a Kitchen in Tokio.

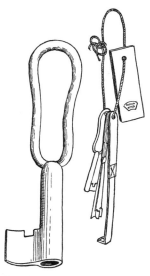

Fig. 141. — Key to Kura, and Bunch of Keys.

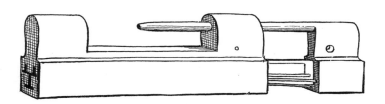

Fig. 142. — Padlock to Kura.

Fig. 143. — Panelled Ceiling.

Fig. 144. — Ramma in Hakóne Village.

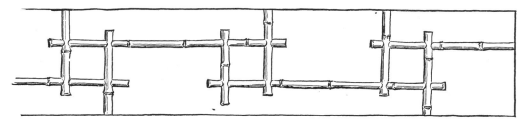
Fig. 145. — Bamboo Ramma.

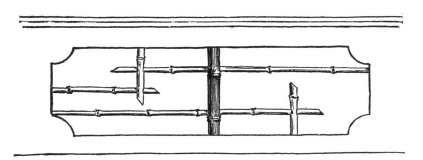
Fig. 146. — Porcelain Ramma, in Tokio.

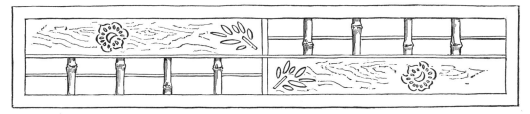
Fig. 147. — Ramma of Bamboo and Perforated Panel.

Fig. 148. — Carved-wood Ramma in Gojio Village, Yamato.

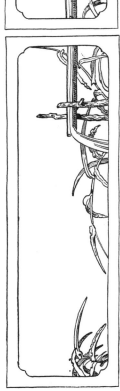

Fig. 149. — Carved-wood Ramma in Town of Yatsushiro, Higo.

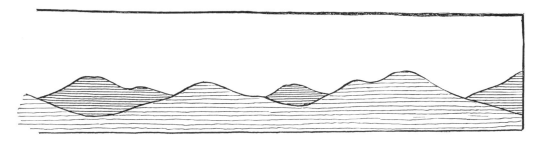

Fig. 150. — Ramma, composed of two Thin Boards, in Nagoya, Owari.

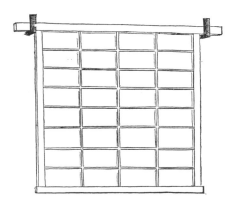

Fig. 151. — Shōji for Window.

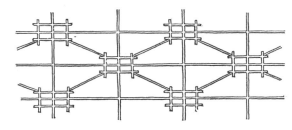

Fig. 152. — Shōji-frame for Window.

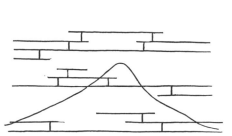

Fig. 153. — Shōji-frame for Window.

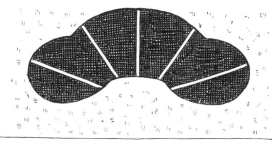

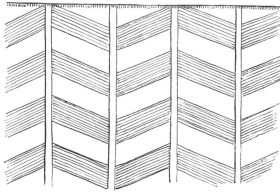

Fig. 154. — Window.

Fig. 155 — Biyō-bu, or Folding Screen.

Fig. 156 Wrought metallic mounting of Screen Frame.

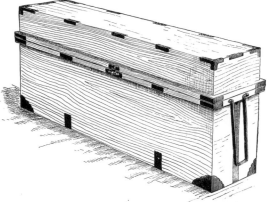

Fig. 157. — Screen-box.

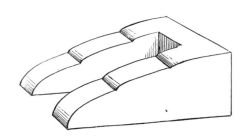

Fig. 158. — Foot-weight for Screen.

Fig. 159. — Furosaki Biyō-bu.

Fig. 160. — Model of Tsui-tate in Pottery.

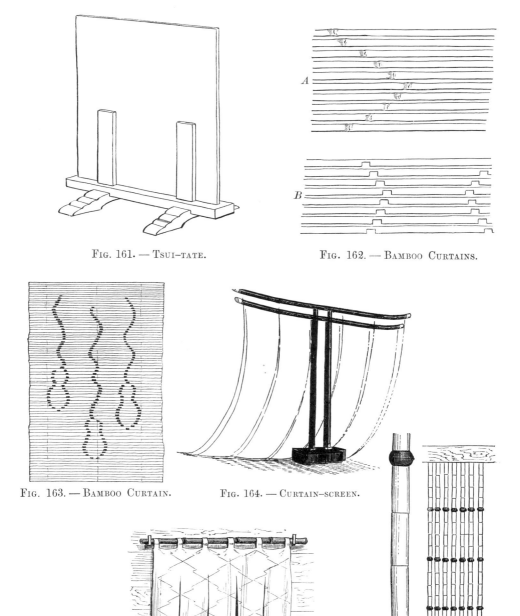

Fig. 161. — Tsui-tate.

Fig. 162. — Bamboo Curtains.

Fig. 163. — Bamboo Curtain.

Fig. 164. — Curtain-screen.

Fig. 165. — Fringed Curtain.

Fig. 166. — Slashed Curtain.

Fig. 167. — Kitchen in old Farmhouse at Kabutoyama.

FIG. 168. — KITCHEN RANGE.

FIG. 169. — KITCHEN RANGE, WITH SMOKE-CONDUCTOR.

Fig. 170. — Kitchen in City House.

Fig. 171. — Braziers.

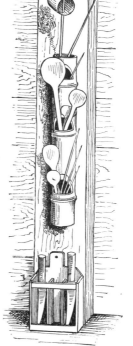

172. — Bamboo Rack and Knife-case.

Fig. 173. — Ji-zai.

Fig. 174. — Fireplace in Country House.

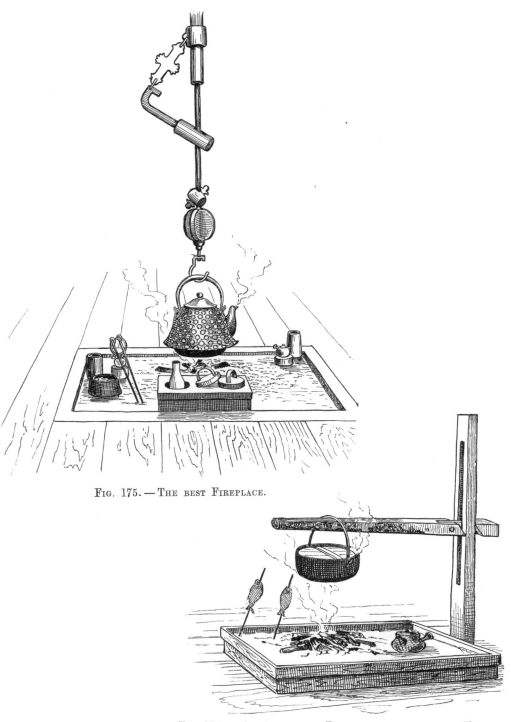

Fig. 175. — The best Fireplace.

Fig. 176. — An Adjustable Device for supporting a Kettle.

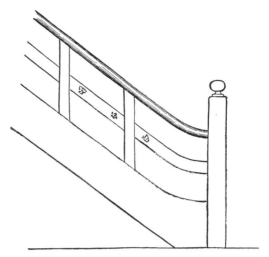

Fig. 178. — Stair-rail.

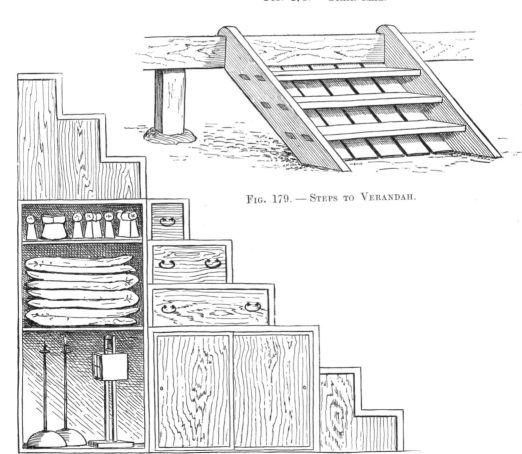

Fig. 179. — Steps to Verandah.

Fig. 177. — Kitchen Closet, Drawers, Cupboard, and Stairs combined.

Fig. 180. — Bath-tub with Side Oven.

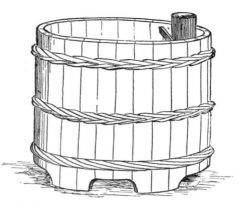

Fig. 181. — Bath-tub with Inside Flue.

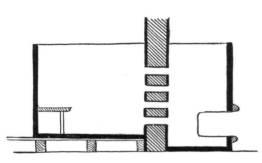

Fig. 182. — Bath-tub in section, with Oven outside the Room.

Fig. 183. — Bath-tub with outside Heating-chamber.

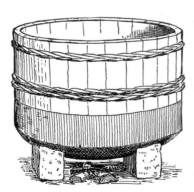

Fig. 184. — Bath-tub, with Iron Base.

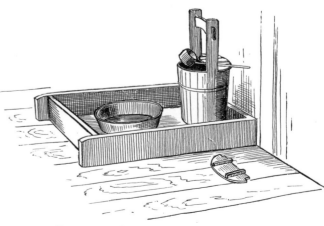

Fig. 185. — Lavatory in Country Inn.

Fig. 186. — Lavatory in Private House.

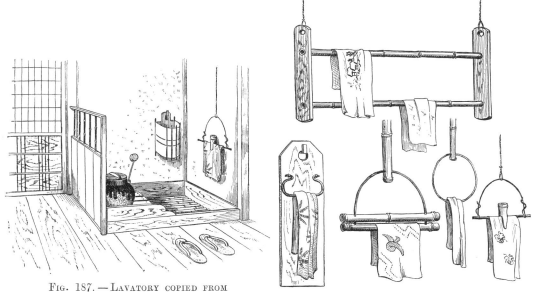

Fig. 187. — Lavatory copied from Japanese Book.

Figs. 188–192. — Forms of Towel-racks.

Fig. 193. — Forms of Pillow in common use.

Fig. 194. — Showing position of Head in resting on Pillow.

Fig. 195. — Heating Arrangement in Floor.

Fig. 196. — Elbow-rest.

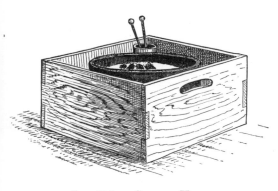

Fig. 197. — Common Hibachi.

Fig. 198. — Hibachi.

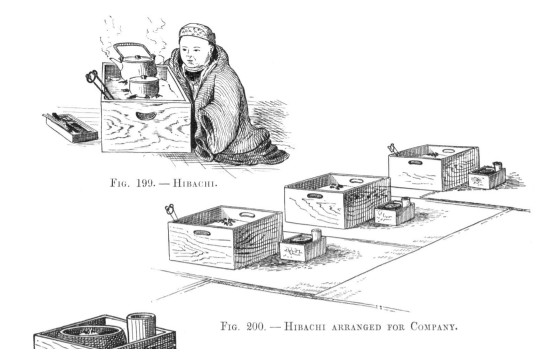

Fig. 199. — Hibachi.

Fig. 200. — Hibachi arranged for Company.

Fig. 201. — Tabako-bon.

Fig. 202. — Tabako-bon.

Fig. 203. — Tabako-bon.

Fig. 204. — Pan for holding burning Charcoal.

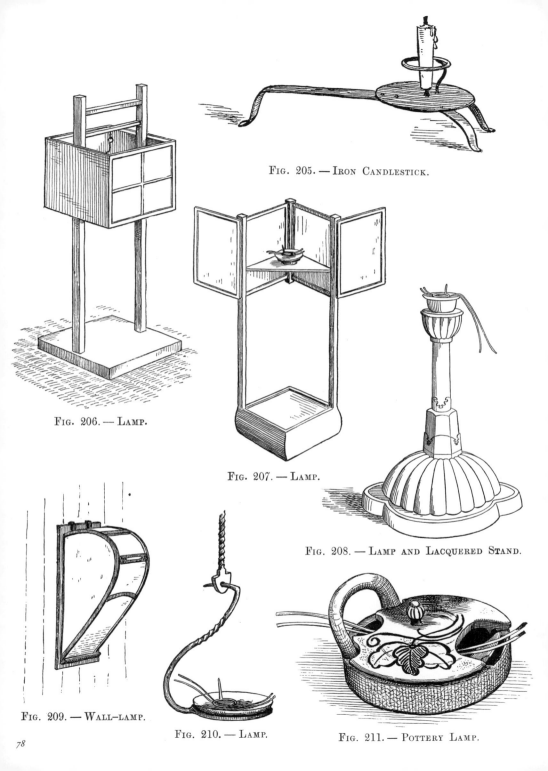

Fig. 205.—Iron Candlestick.

Fig. 206.—Lamp.

Fig. 207.—Lamp.

Fig. 208.—Lamp and Lacquered Stand.

Fig. 209.—Wall-lamp.

Fig. 210.—Lamp.

Fig. 211.—Pottery Lamp.

Fig. 212. — Pottery Lamp.

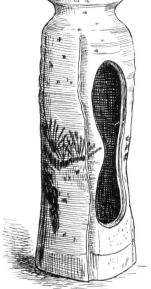

Fig. 213. — Pottery Candle-stick.

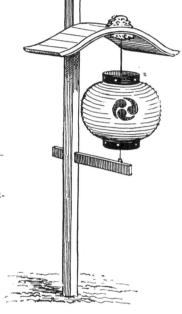

Fig. 214. — Fixed Street-lantern.

Fig. 215. — Household Shrine.

Fig. 216. — Swallows' Nests in Private House.

Fig. 217. — Interior of Privy.

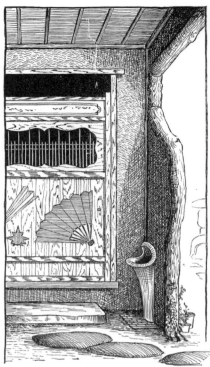

Fig. 219. — Privy connected with a Merchant's House in Asakusa.

Fig. 220. — Interior of a Privy in Asakusa.

Fig. 218. — Privy of Inn in Hachi-ishi Village, Nikko.

Fig. 221. — Main Entrance to House.

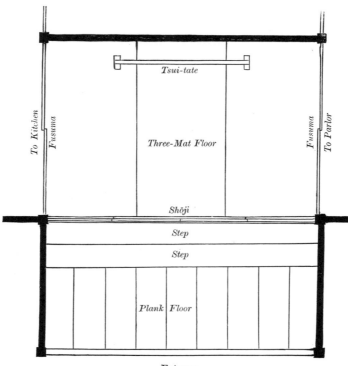

Fig. 222. — Plan of Vestibule and Hall.

Fig. 223. — Shoe-closet.

Fig. 224. — Lantern-shelf in Hall.

Fig. 225. — Grated Entrance, with Sliding Door.

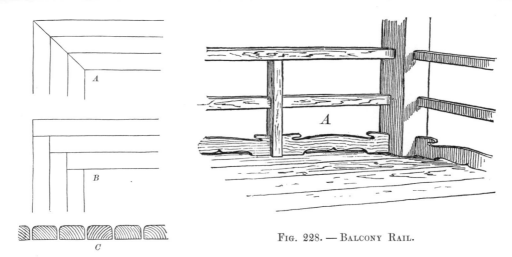

Fig. 226. — Verandah Floor.

Fig. 228. — Balcony Rail.

Fig. 227. — Verandah of an old Kioto House.

Fig. 229. — Balcony Rail and Perforated Panels.

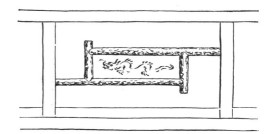

Fig. 230. — Balcony Rail.

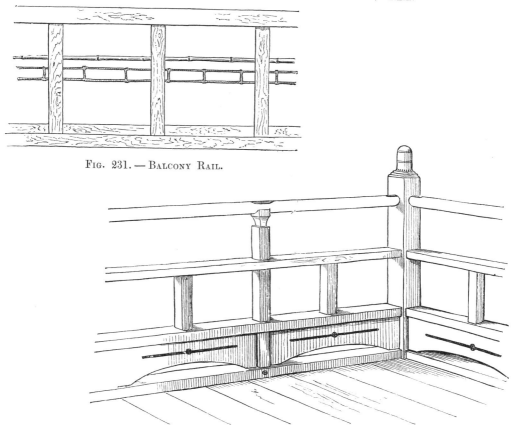

Fig. 231. — Balcony Rail.

Fig. 232. — Balcony Rail.

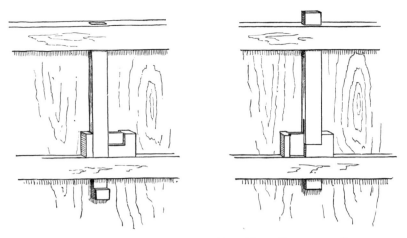

Fig. 233. — Rain-door Lock unbolted.   Fig. 234. — Rain-door Lock bolted.

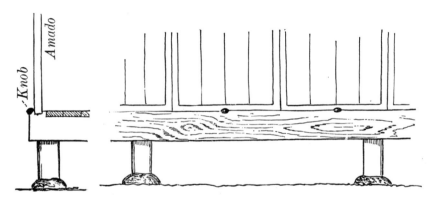

Fig. 235. — Knob for Rain-door.

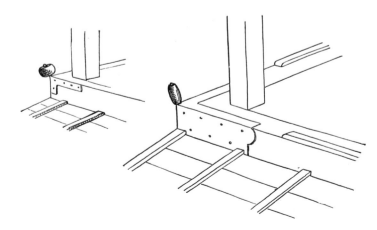

Fig. 236. — Corner-roller for Rain-door.

Fig. 237. — Verandah showing Swinging Closet for Rain-doors, and also Chōdzu-bachi.

Fig. 239. — Chōdzu-bachi.

Fig. 238. Chōdzu-bachi.

Fig. 240. — Chōdzu-bachi.

Fig. 241. — Chōdzu-bachi and Hisashi-yen.

Fig. 243. — Gateway of City House from within.

Fig. 242. — Gateway in Yashiki Building.

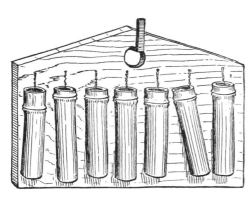

Fig. 244. — Gate-rattle.

Fig. 245. — Bolt for little Sliding Door in Gateway.

Fig. 246. — Gateway to City Residence.

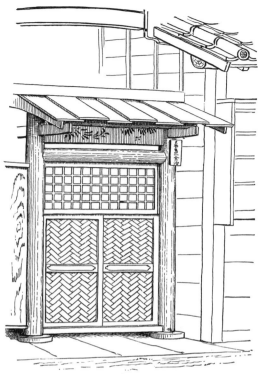

Fig. 247. — Gateway to City Residence.

Fig. 249. — Gateway.

Fig. 248. — Gateway near Tokio.

Fig. 250. — Rustic Gateway.

Fig. 251. — Rustic Gateway.

Fig. 252. — Rustic Garden Gate.

Fig. 253. — Garden Gateway.

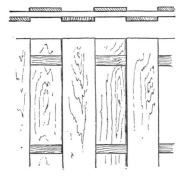

Fig. 254.—Ordinary Wooden Fence.

Fig. 255.—Stake Fence.

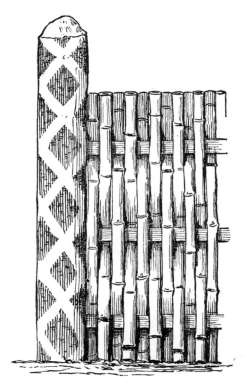

Fig. 256.—Bamboo Fence.

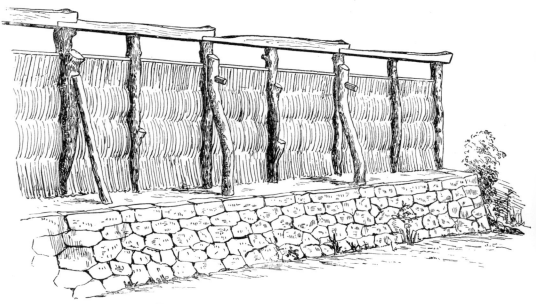

Fig. 257.—Fence in Hakóne Village.

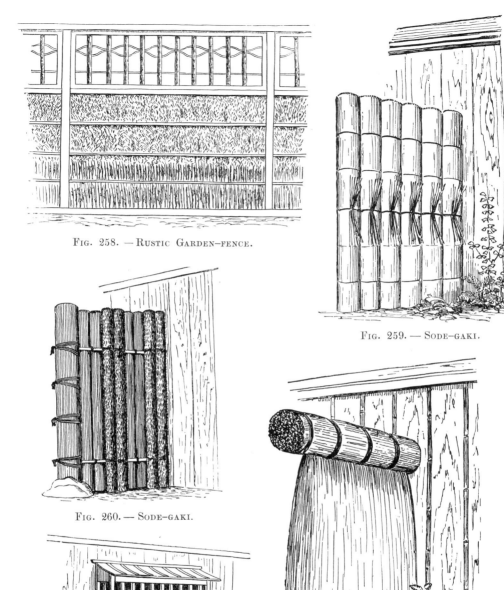

Fig. 258. — Rustic Garden-fence.

Fig. 259. — Sode-gaki.

Fig. 260. — Sode-gaki.

Fig. 261. — Sode-gaki.

Fig. 262. — Barred Opening in Fence.

Fig. 263. — Garden Tablet.

Fig. 264. Ishi-dōrō in Tokio.

Fig. 265. — Ishi-dōrō in Miyajima.

Fig. 266. — Ishi-dōrō in Shirako, Musashi.

Fig. 267. — Ishi-dōrō in Utsunomiya.

Fig. 268. — Stone Foot-bridge.

Fig. 269. — Stone Foot-bridge.

Fig. 270. — Garden Brook and Foot-bridge.

Fig 272. — Summer-house in Imperial Garden, Tokio.

Fig. 271. — Summer-house in Private Garden, Tokio.

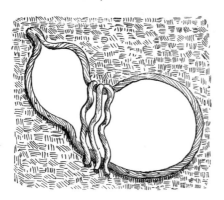

Fig. 273. — Rustic Opening in Summer-house, Kobe.

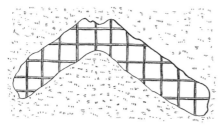

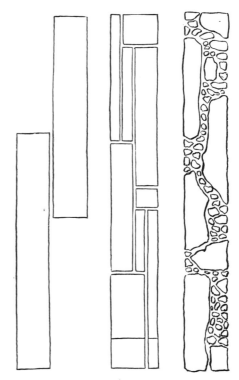

Fig. 274. — Rustic Opening in Summer-house, Okazaki.

Fig. 275. — Various Forms of Garden Paths.

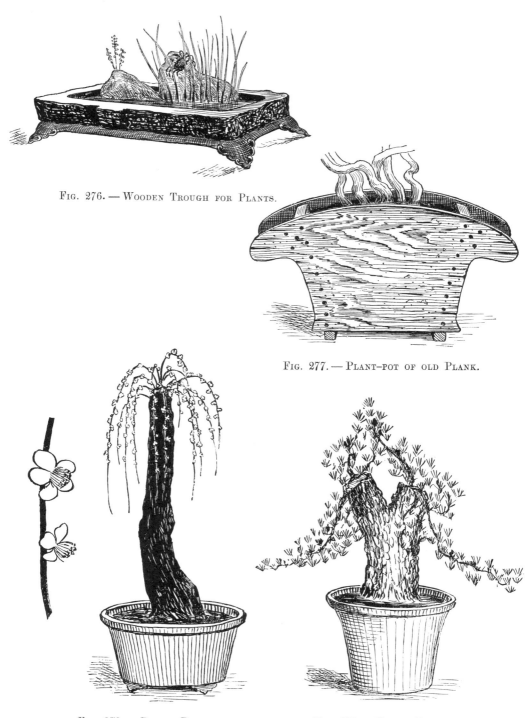

Fig. 276. — Wooden Trough for Plants.

Fig. 277. — Plant-pot of old Plank.

Fig. 278. — Dwarf Plum.

Fig. 279. — Dwarf Pine.

Fig. 280. — Curiously trained Pine-tree.

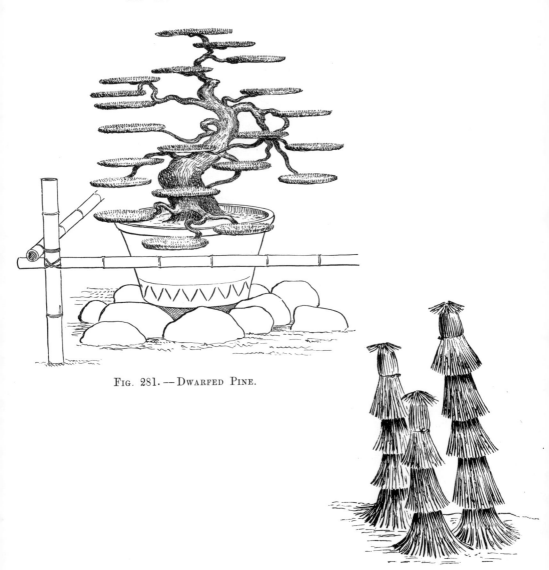

Fig. 281. — Dwarfed Pine.

Fig. 282. — Shrubs wrapped in Straw for Winter.

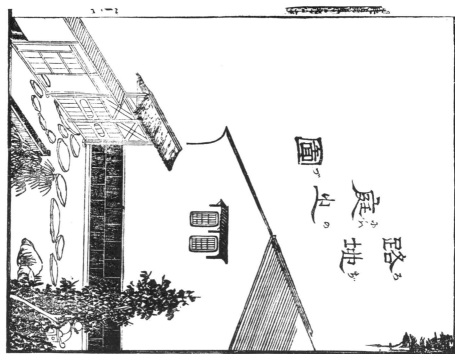

Fig. 283, Showing Approaches to House. (Reproduced from "Chikusan Teizoden," a Japanese Work.)

FIG. 284. — LITTLE GARDEN BELONGING TO THE PRIESTS OF A BUDDHIST TEMPLE.
(REPRODUCED FROM "CHIKUSAN TEIZODEN," A JAPANESE WORK.)

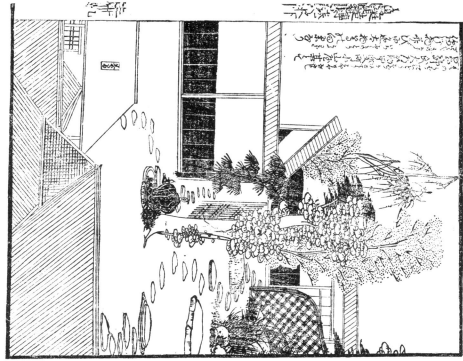
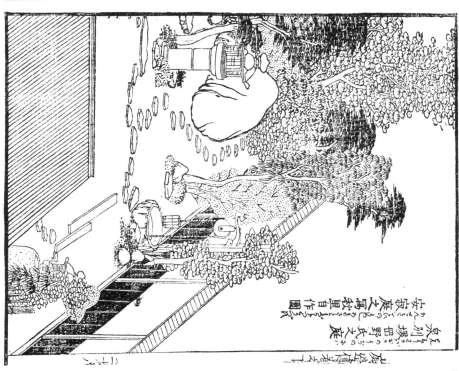

Fig. 285. — Garden of a Merchant. (Reproduced from "Chikusan Teizoden," a Japanese Work.)

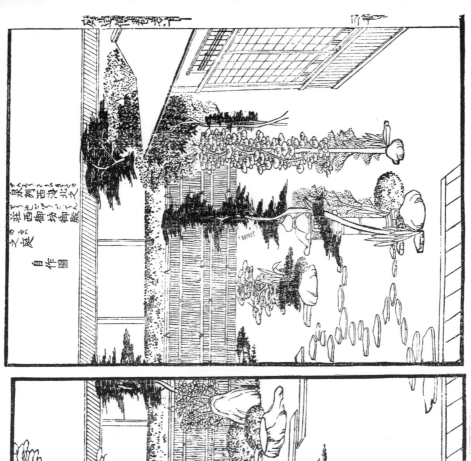

FIG. 286. — GARDEN OF A DAIMIO. (REPRODUCED FROM "CHIKUSAN TEIZODEN," A JAPANESE WORK.)

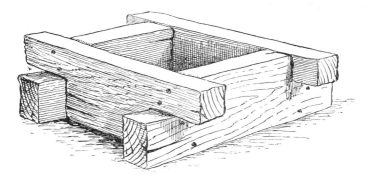

Fig. 287. — Ancient Form of Well-curb.

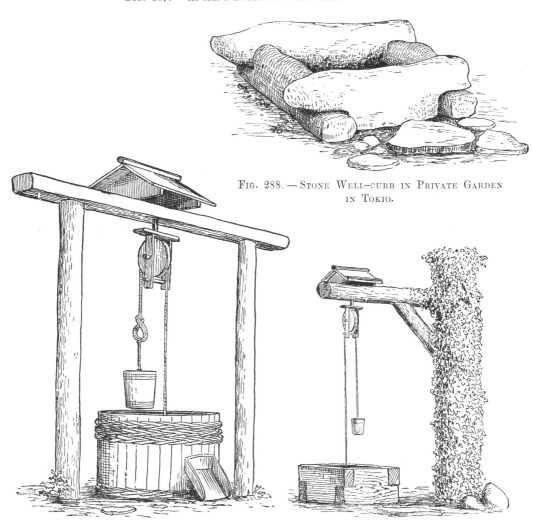

Fig. 288. — Stone Well-curb in Private Garden in Tokio.

Fig. 289. — Wooden Well-frame.

Fig. 290. — Rustic Well-frame.

Fig. 291. — Aqueduct Reservoir at Miyajima, Aki.

Fig. 293. — Well in Kaga Yashiki, Tokio.

Fig. 292. — Aqueducts at Miyajima, Aki.

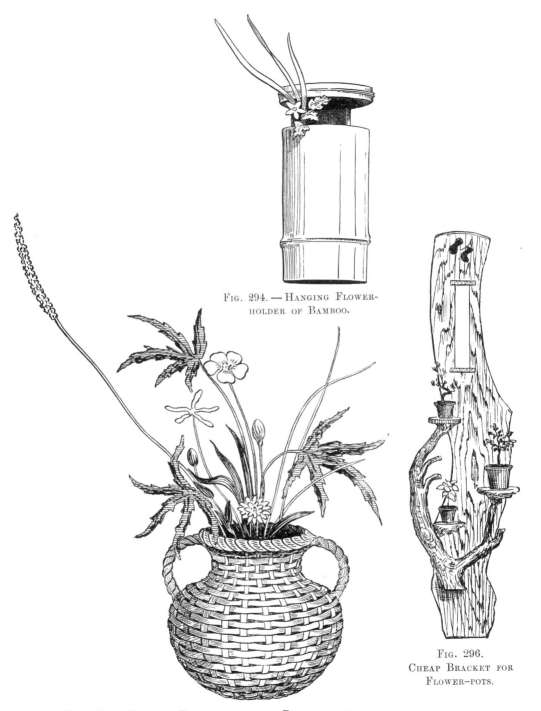

Fig. 294. — Hanging Flower-holder of Bamboo.

Fig. 295. — Hanging Flower-holder of Basket-work.

Fig. 296. Cheap Bracket for Flower-pots.

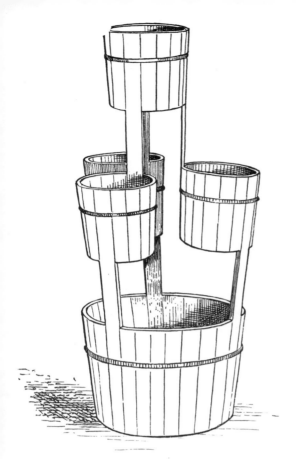

Fig. 297. — Curious Combination of Buckets for Flowers.

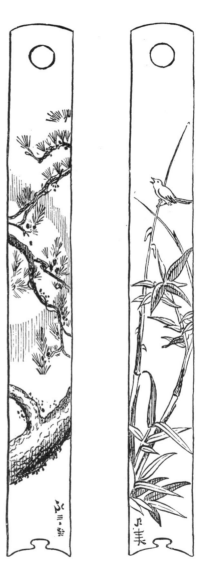

Fig. 299. — Hashira-kakushi.

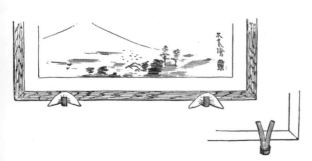

Fig. 298. — Framed Picture, with Supports.

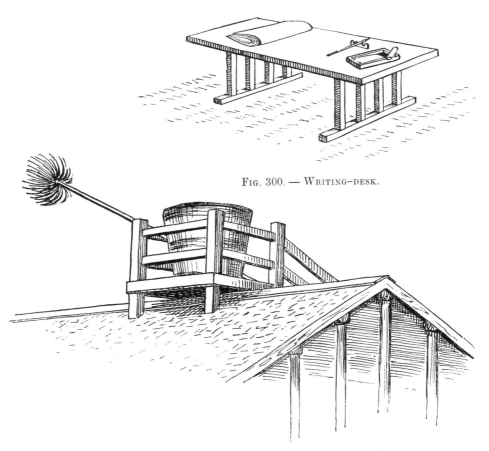

Fig. 300. — Writing-desk.

Fig. 301. — Staging on House-roof, with Bucket and Brush.

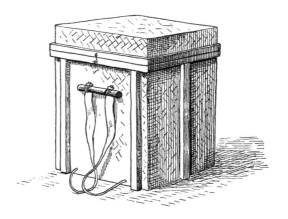

Fig. 302. — Box for Transporting Articles.

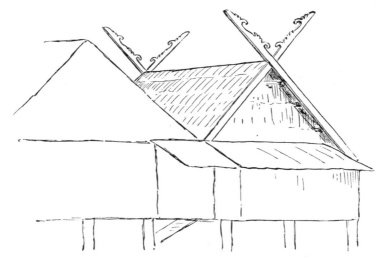

Fig. 303. — Malay House near Singapore.

Fig. 304. — Ridge of Roof in Cholon, Anam.

Fig. 305. — Interior of Malay House, showing Bed-place. Singapore.

Fig. 306. — Aino House, Yezo.

Fig. 307. — Aino House, Yezo.

図版解説

原著図版キャプションに本文内容や最新の情報も加味して訳出しました。

〈街と村の風景〉
図1　東京の風景、店舗と住宅が隙間なく建ち並んでいる（写真から作成）。
図2　東京の風景、寺と庭に多くの樹木が植えられて自然が都市の中に取り込まれている（写真から作成）。
図3　小さな家屋が密集している、江の島〔神奈川県藤沢市〕の風景（写真から作成）。

〈住まいの建て方〉
図4　壁の骨組。柱にうがたれた柄穴（ほぞあな）に短材が差し込まれて楔（くさび）で固定されている。
図5　数人がかりで、礎石を打ち込んでいるところ。
図6　礎石（土台石）。
図7　骨組の断面。梁（はり）には素朴な丸太や不整形なものが見られる。
図8　切妻（きりづま）屋根の骨組。
図9　大きな建物の妻面の骨組、小屋組。
図10　大きな建物の屋根の小屋組。
図11　蔵の小屋組。
図12　一般的な2階建て住宅の骨組。H：柱、D：土台、DI：土台石（礎石）、M：間柱、N：貫、Ni：2階梁、Ya：屋根下、T：垂木、Yu：床下、Ne：根太丸太。
図13　建物外部の補強、2本の控え柱で柱を補強している。
図14　外部の補強材、腕木（うでぎ）。
図15　装飾的な腕木。
図16　住宅用材の割り方。
図17　丸い床柱に溝を彫って、隔壁を嵌め込んだところの横断面。
図18　板材を束ねたもの。
図19　天井の断面。
図20　天井の竿縁（さおぶち）を仮支えているところ。
図21　上から見た天井の支え方。
図22　石で押さえられた天井板。
図23　押入れの天井板。
図24　木目をそろえるための、板束からの板の取り出し方。
図25　正方形の瓦による外壁の配列。

〈大工道具など〉

図26　日本の大工の万力の使い方。
図27　よく使われる大工道具。A：手斧（ちょうな）、B, C：鋸（のこぎり）、D, E：鉋（かんな）。
図28　携帯用の釘箱、腰の帯などに吊り下げて使う。
図29　両端が刷毛状になった木製の筆記具、墨刺（すみさし）。
図30　墨壺（すみつぼ）。
図31　下げ振り。
図32　昔の大工（古い絵から写す）。道具箱のふたに片手用の手鋸が付いている。

〈都市と郊外の民家〉

図33　通りに並ぶ家々、東京・神田〔東京都千代田区〕。木の格子の出窓、門構えの出入り口……。
図34　図33と同じ通りに並んで建つ2軒の家。よく整備された溝が路肩に設けられ、出入り口には小さな木の橋が渡されている。
図35　明治維新以後、東京に現われた粗末な平屋建の長屋（ながや）。
図36　東京に新しく開かれた住宅地の通りから眺めた、中流の2階建て住宅。2階の窓には簾（すだれ）がかかっている。
図37　図36の住宅を、庭から眺める。居室は横一列に並んでいて、広い縁側越しに庭に面している。図98の間取り（平面図）参照。
図38　平屋の住宅、東京・九段〔東京都千代田区〕。瓦屋根の妻面が奇妙な形をしている。溝を渡った玄関には格子の引戸、大きな出窓にも格子、塀の上部に簾が見え、縁側や庭があることを思わせる。
図39　陸前・松島〔宮城県〕近くの宿屋。重量感のある曲がった木の梁（はり）、軒の板屋根は石で押えられ、茅葺き（かやぶき）屋根には煙出しが見える。
図40　図39と同じ陸前地方の別の宿屋。煙出しは屋根の上に小屋根をかたどって造られている。
図41　蝦夷・室蘭〔北海道〕の家。並はずれて大きく広い屋根、煙出しは棟の上に付属屋として造られ、平らな棟には赤いユリが植えられている。
図42　深い軒の出を持つ切妻の壁から突き出した、陸前・オヅカ（宮城県大塚？）村の出窓には、交互に松と竹をあしらった透かし彫りの板が嵌め込まれている。
図43　陸中〔岩手県〕の3階建ての宿屋。
図44　街道に妻側を向けて並ぶ茅葺きの家、道との境には背の高い竹垣、盛岡郊外。
図45　武蔵・冑山（かぶとやま）〔埼玉県熊谷市〕の古くからの農家。母屋の右端には分厚い茅葺き屋根を持つ建物が妻壁を向けて突き出ている。図85参照。
図46　京都の古い民家。通りから見たもので、重々しい屋根の門。外壁は漆喰（しっくい）で、小さな格子窓がいくつも付いている。
図47　図46の京都の家の門を入ったところから見た、中庭の眺め。住居の茅葺き屋根は急勾配で、棟は瓦で葺かれている。

図48　図46・47の京都の家の裏庭からの眺め。住まいは庭に向かって開放的で室内から庭や池を見渡せる。

図49　東京のとある陶器店の住まい。縁側の奥はかわやで、外から出入りするため草履が置かれている。目隠しの袖壁（そでかべ）には古い舟板が使われており、太い竹の棒で家に取り付けられている。水をためた陶製の手水鉢の先にも袖壁があり、これは台所の庭との仕切りになっている。

図50　2階から眺めた住宅のたたずまい、東京・今戸〔東京都台東区〕の隅田川沿いの家。ブラシ状の短い袖壁が斜めに突き出し、外と出入りする木戸と家との仕切りになっている。縁側や2階のバルコニーの様子がよくわかり、庇が有効に働いていることも見てとれる。

図51　駿河・三島〔静岡県〕の古い宿屋。2階が1階よりも前に出て、軒も深く突き出す独特の形態で、側面の飾り板も異彩を放っている。

図52　山城・長池〔京都府城陽市〕の村の通り。京都と奈良を結ぶ街道沿い、手前は旅人の休息のための茶店、隣はロウソク屋、人力車屋、と続いている。

図53　大隅・元垂水〔鹿児島県垂水市〕の海岸。

図54　図53の集落の家。屋根の棟は何層もの竹で覆われ、屋外の井戸には大きな跳ね釣瓶（つるべ）がある。

図55　函館の漁師小屋。背の高い防風柵が、荒れ狂う海風から小屋を守っている。

図56　江の島の漁師の集落。

図57　東京の骨董商の蔵。蔵とは耐火建築物のことで、大事な古書や古美術品が保管されている。

図58　東京の古物商の蔵。図57同様、貴重な品がおさめられている。

図59　函館の古い家。中央の2階建ての蔵の周りを瓦屋根の増築部が囲んでおり、ここは家族の住まいになっている。

〈板屋根 など〉

図60　庇（ひさし）、主屋根の軒下から突き出ている差し掛け屋根で、幅広の薄い板でできている。

図61　板屋根の材料と道具。A：柿板（こけらいた）の束、B・C：屋根職人が使うハンマー、b：刻みの入った真鍮（しんちゅう）製の細い板、D：竹釘。

図62　屋根葺き職人のハンマーの握り方。

図63　板屋根の竹押え。細長い割竹を棟木から軒先まで斜めに渡すことで、屋根板が強風ではがされるのを防いでいる。

図64　作業途中の柿葺き（こけらぶき）の板屋根。A：二つに仕切られた釘箱、大きい方には竹釘、小さい方には金釘が入っている。B：柿板を何枚も深く重ねた高級な柿葺き屋根、軒先にはくさび形の木片が仕込まれて優美な反りを作っている。

図65　柿葺き屋根の棟。柿板を5〜6層重ねて固定し、木や竹の細長い材を2本釘止めして押さえている。

図66　雨樋（あまどい）。屋根からの雨水は細長い竹の節を抜いて割った横樋（とい）

が受け、竪樋で支えられている四角い箱状のものに導かれる。竪樋も竹の節をくりぬいて作られたもので、その上端は四つに切り込まれて穴の開いた四角い箱を固定している。

〈**瓦屋根** など〉
図67　瓦屋根の棟。家を火から守りたいという願いからか、水をテーマとしたデザインを多く見かける。茅葺き屋根の棟にも「水」という漢字を意匠化したものが黒くワラに刻まれているものがある（図82 参照）。
図68-70　笠木瓦を使った壁の装飾、大和〔奈良県〕。
図71　瓦屋根の軒先、軒瓦には装飾性が求められ、その細長い部分には花や渦巻きなどの伝統的な意匠の浮き彫りが、また丸い部分には家紋が描かれることが多い。
図72-A　長崎の本瓦屋根。ゆるやかなカーブを持つ凸面を下にし、その上に半円筒形の瓦の凸面を上にして、下の瓦の継ぎ目を覆うようにしたもの。B：軒先瓦の改良形で、日本の南部やジャワ〔インドネシア〕で見受けられる。
図73　東京の本瓦屋根の軒先。家紋が描かれることが多いが、徳川家の三つ葉葵紋を見かけることはめったにない。
図74　江戸瓦で葺いた屋根の軒瓦。
図75　フランス瓦の軒先。日本に招来されてまだ間もない新しいタイプの瓦。
図76　石見〔いわみ、島根県〕の棟瓦。A：屋根の形をした瓦で、茅葺き屋根の棟を覆っている。B：本瓦が使われることもある。
図77　日光〔栃木県〕の石屋根。大谷石（おおやいし）を一定の形に切って、順次かさなってつながれてゆく。

〈**茅葺き屋根** など〉
図78　茅葺き（かやぶき）屋根とその道具。A：屋根葺き材には一般的には藁（ワラ）、上等なものには茅（カヤ）が使われる。葺き草は適当なかたまりに束ねられ、向きをそろえて垂木（たるき）に固定して、その上を一時的に竹などで屋根面に押しつける。葺き草が押しつけられているあいだに、独特の形をした木槌（きづち、B）で打ち込み、長い柄の付いたはさみ（C）で端部を刈りそろえる
図79　屋根飾り、磐城・藤田〔福島県国見町〕。丸い棟木が妻面上部に飛び出し、その上に黒く塗られた長い飾り板が取り付けられている。
図80　茅葺き屋根の瓦棟、磐城〔福島県〕。棟の上にスサを混ぜた土や粘土を積み重ね、それを半円筒形の瓦や幅広の本瓦を使って棟の両側から頂上にかけて帽子のようにかぶせたつくり。
図81　茅葺き屋根の瓦棟、武蔵〔埼玉・東京・神奈川の一部〕。図80と同じようなつくりで、瓦のいちばん下を丸竹で押さえている。
図82　茅葺き屋根の竹製の棟飾り、武蔵。棟の表面を小さな竹で層状に覆い、次に目の詰まった幅の狭い竹皮や樹皮で直角方向に棟を巻き、その上を棟に平行に丸竹か割竹で押さえている。

図83　東京近郊の茅葺き屋根。妻破風に三角形の開口部（煙出し）を設けた、美しい造形。北国の茅葺き屋根には煙出しに多くの工夫が見られる（図39・40・41参照）。

図84　東京近郊の茅葺き屋根（写真から作成）。切妻に三角形の煙出しがあり、屋根は切妻と寄棟の性格をあわせ持っている。

図85　図45の武蔵・青山〔埼玉県熊谷市〕の古い農家・茅葺き屋根の棟飾り。小棟が反り上がり、多くのX字形の組木（置き千木）が狭い間隔で載っている。伊勢の神道の社殿、安南〔ヴェトナム〕、シンガポール近郊のマレー人の家屋にも類似のものが見られる。

図86　単純な棟の形の茅葺き屋根、近江〔滋賀県〕。棟と直角方向に薄い板を屋根の流れにそって張り、棟の頂部と下端に細長い板を取り付けて全体を固定している。

図87　竹と瓦の棟を持つ茅葺き屋根、摂津・高槻〔大阪府〕。急角度な棟の表面を目の詰まった竹の編み物（竹簀）で覆い、さらに瓦を棟にそって一定間隔で置いている。

図88　寄棟屋根の上に棟屋根（棟飾り）を載せた茅葺き屋根、三河〔愛知県〕。急勾配の棟屋根の表面には薄い樹皮を棟と直行して張り付け、その上を棟と平行に数本の竹を取り付けて押さえる。さらにその上を半円筒形の太い目蓋（めぶた）を直行して載せて固定する。棟の頂部には1本の長い竹が置かれ、目蓋と目蓋の間で棟に結び付けられている。妻面の煙出しはワラの覆いによって保護されていて、中から煙は出ても雨は中に入ってこないようになっている。

図89　茅葺き屋根の棟飾り、京都。図88と同様のつくりの屋根と棟飾りを持つが、煙出しには重厚な格子が付いている。

図90　太い竹で覆われた棟飾りを持つ茅葺き屋根、三河〔愛知県〕。

図91　茅葺き屋根の棟飾り、紀伊〔和歌山県〕。図88と類似のつくりだが、目蓋は棟の頂部では細く、先にゆくにしたがって太くなっている。また煙出しは小さい。

図92　茅葺き屋根の棟飾り、大和〔奈良県〕。切妻の妻壁は粘土とスサを混ぜてつくられ、屋根よりも30センチ以上高く立ち上がり、上には瓦が載っている。

図93　茅葺き屋根の棟飾り、遠江〔静岡県〕。他の地方では見かけない独特のつくり。棟飾りは大きく急勾配で、棟に平行に数多くの竹で覆われ、その上を直行する幅広い目蓋で押さえられ、そのまた上を平行する2本の太い竹で固定されれている。また棟の頂部は半分に割った竹を曲げたものを使って、目蓋の間で挟むようにして留められている。

図94　茅葺き屋根の棟飾り、伊勢〔三重県〕。単純なつくりで棟飾りは低く、その表面は樹皮で覆われたうえに、竹で固定されている。

図95　茅葺き屋根の軒下まわり。軒樋や竪樋を付けられない茅葺き屋根の軒下では、雨だれを受けるために玉砂利が敷かれることが多い。

〈室内・間取り・畳・引戸 など〉

図96　鉢石〔栃木県日光市〕の客間。

図97　明治初期に東京に新築された家の間取り。P：応接間または客間（8畳）、S：居間（4畳半）、D：食堂（6畳）、L：図書室（6畳）、St：書斎（3畳）、SR：女中部屋（2畳）、

B：寝室（3畳）、K：台所、H：玄関の間（3畳）、V：玄関のタタキ（2畳）、C：押入れ、T：床の間、Sh：神棚、U and L：かわや。2本の平行線は建具（襖・障子・雨戸など）、黒く太い線は壁を示す。密な平行線は縁側、まばらな平行線は台所・風呂・通路など。斜線部は中央の溝に向かって板敷きの床が傾斜しており、陶製の水桶か木製の風呂桶が置いてある。屋外に出ている濃い斜線部は戸袋。各部屋は畳敷きで、家具はほとんどない。

図 98　東京のある家（図 36・37）の間取り。P：応接間または客間（8畳）、B：寝室（8畳と6畳）、S：居間（4畳半）、K：台所、SR：女中部屋（3畳）、BR：風呂、E：勝手口、V：玄関のタタキ、H：玄関の間（3畳）、WR：待合（4畳半）、C：押入れ、T：床の間、U and L：かわや。図面の表現は図 97 と同じ。

図 99　大名屋敷（部分）の平面図。大名が公式の客を迎える部屋は数センチ高くなった上段の間で、入側（いりかわ）と呼ばれる緩衝空間（廊下）に取り巻かれている。図中の密な平行線は縁側（濡れ縁）。太い実線は壁、細い線は障子や襖、四角い黒点は柱を示す。Agari-ba 上がり場：風呂に出入りするときに使う所、Cha-dokoro 茶所：茶を供する所、Ge-dan 下段：低い段、Jo-dan 上段：高い段、Iri-kawa 入側：縁側と部屋との間の空間、Kami-no-ma 上の間：上方（じょうほう）の部屋、Tsugi-no-ma 次の間：その次の部屋、Kesho-no-ma 化粧の間：化粧室、Nan-do 納戸：物置、Naka-tsubo 中壺：中間の空間、Oshi-ire 押入れ：戸棚、Ro-ka 廊下：歩廊・屋根のある通路、Tamari 溜り：控えの部屋、Tsume-sho 詰所：召使いの控え所、Yu-dono 湯殿：風呂、Yen-zashiki 縁座敷：はずれの客間、Watari 渡り：渡ること、Sunoko 簀子：竹製の棚または床（ゆか）。

図 100　畳。

図 101　異なる大きさの部屋での畳の敷き方。

図 102　畳の上での女性の座り姿勢。

図 103　縁側と客間の断面図。

図 104　葦戸（よしど）。葭障子（よししょうじ）、簾障子（すだれしょうじ）ともいう。

図 105　引戸。玄関から家の中に入る開口部にはめられており、軽い黒竹と木目のよく見える杉板を組み合わせて、仕上げられている。

図 106　襖の引手。ある貴族の家のもので、硯と筆があしらわれ、くぼみには龍が彫られている。

図 107　襖の引手。銅製で釉薬がかけられ、木の葉は緑、木の実は赤と白に彩色されている。

図 108 – 109　襖の引手。手彫りではなく模様を印刷した安物だが、凝ったデザインが施されている。

図 110　ひも付の引手。古い時代の貴族や大名の家に見られるもので、古本から模写した。

図 111　障子の桟（さん）の矯正。組子がゆがんだときなど、竹の枝を桟の対角線上に差し込み、そのしなりでゆがみを直す。

図 112　障子の桟の装飾。

図 113　床柱の一部。面を削るようにして八角形に仕上げてある。

図114-117　装飾用の飾り釘。床柱と落掛け（おとしがけ）を留めるところに使われる。
図118　霞や雲をかたどった違い棚。上は一般的な棚の形の略図、下は伝統的な雲形。

〈床の間と違い棚を見せるインテリア〉
図119　位の高い貴族の住まいの客間。縁側越しに庭に面した開放的な部屋で、違い棚と平行に並んだ床の間は、間口が広く大きい。
図120　部屋のコーナーにくぼみのある客間、図119の隣の部屋。床の間と違い棚が部屋の隅に直角に並んでいる。床の間の右の壁には引き分け障子の付いた円窓（まるまど）があり、その上の細長い長方形の窓にの障子があって通風のために開けられたりする。違い棚の左には引違い戸の付いた奥行きの深い地袋があり、その上には装飾性のある障子がある。
図121　円窓を見せる客間。床の間と縁側の間に壁が設けられて、その中央に優美な竹細工が施された大きな円窓がある。床の間の前に座った客は、外からの直射日光や風から守られ、障子越しの明りも得られるし、障子を開けて庭を眺めることもできる。
図122　書院のある客間。図121と似たつくりだが、窓は火灯窓（花頭窓、かとうまど）で地袋の付いた棚を持つ書院となっていて、棚の上に筆などの文筆具が置かれている。
図123　幅広の床の間がある客間。部屋の一面すべてを床の間が占め、違い棚は隅に置かれ、地袋は三角形に縮小されている。
図124　小規模な客間。床の間はあるが、違い棚はない。床の間の明かり取りの窓も小さく控えめ。床柱が大きく切り取られ、構造的には問題があるが、奇妙な効果を生んでいる。
図125　簡素な客間。床の間は部屋の隅で縁側と直行し、違い棚との境の壁に縦長の開口部が開けられ、明かり取りになっている。
図126　京都・清水の2階の客間。太めの床柱は美しくねじれ、樹皮を剝いて磨き上げられている。天井は正方形の古い杉の板目が美しい。
図127　東京の住宅の客間。床の間や違い棚は華やかで、仕切り壁は取り払われて壁面に柱が取り付けられているだけ。天井は網代につくられているなど、細かいところまで工夫されていて魅力的な部屋である。
図128　農家の客間。田舎の庶民の部屋で簡素なものだが、床の間には仕切りのある垂れ壁や、古い難破船から持ってきたという黒い板の棚などが設けられている。床の間の床面は少し高くなっているが、違い棚の床面は畳面と同じ。
図129　客間の隅で、床の間と障子が接する部分の長押（なげし）のおさめ方。

〈茶　室〉
図130　京都・南禅寺の茶室、小堀遠州の作といわれる名席。南禅寺塔頭（たっちゅう）金地院にあり、窓が多いことから八窓の席と呼ばれる。広さは三畳台目。
図131　名古屋・富士見陶房の茶室。天井は柿板（こけらいた）を編んだもので、横木や柱には竹や赤松が使われている。炉が三角に切られているのも珍しい。
図132　宮島〔広島県〕の茶室。炉は円形で、板張りの中にある。

図133　茶事のための台所、東京・今戸〔東京都台東区〕。茶室の隣にあって、茶道具を整理保管し、茶事の準備にも使われる部屋。水屋。
図134　東京・今戸の茶室。主人が中国風を意識して造ったものという。1本の太い竹で弧を描いて二分された天井は、片方は木目の美しい杉板を使った大きな正方形、もう一方は小さな杉板が配されている。その他の細部にも凝った趣向が見受けられる。
図135　図134の茶室の反対側の隅を眺めたところ。

〈蔵のインテリア など〉
図136　古い商家の2階の部屋、武蔵・川越〔埼玉県〕。築300年以上という。
図137　蔵を書物部屋にしている例、東京。図57のいちばん端の建物の1階。分厚い壁は冷たく湿気ることがあるので、竹で簡単な枠組みを作り、それを壁から1メートルほど離して立て、カーテンのような垂れ布を張って、壁面や上階の根太隠している。
図138　垂れ布の部屋をつくるための枠組。180年前に出版された書籍からの模写。
図139　蔵と住まいをつなぐ空間、東京。母屋と蔵は5メートルほど離れており、そこに屋根がかけられて台所として使われている。
図140　京都の古い蔵の入口。蔵の扉はぶ厚く重く、通常は換気のために開けられているが、丈夫な格子戸で入口は閉じられている。
図141　蔵の鍵と鍵束。大きな鍵は、蔵の内側の格子戸のもの。
図142　蔵の南京錠。蔵の外側の戸のもの。

〈天井・欄間・窓〉
図143　板張り天井。ふつうに見かけるもので、大きな正方形の杉板が竹やケヤキで縁どられている。
図144　古い家の欄間模様、箱根村〔神奈川県箱根町〕。
図145　竹製の欄間。
図146　陶磁器製の欄間
図147　竹と透かし彫り板の欄間。
図148　木彫りの欄間、大和・五條村〔奈良県五條市〕。
図149　木彫りの欄間、肥後・八代〔熊本県八代市〕。
図150　2枚の薄板で作られた欄間、尾張・名古屋〔愛知県名古屋市〕。
図151　窓の外にかけられる障子。障子の枠の上框（うわがまち）が突き出していて、壁にある鉄の留め金に引っかける。
図152　障子の組子、幾何学模様。
図153　障子の組子、山のかたちを表現したものも多い。
図154　書院の窓、竪格子は鉄製で開口部は杉板と白木を交互に組み合わせたもの。

〈屏風・衝立・簾・暖簾 など〉
図155　屏風（びょうぶ）、図は狩野常信が冬景色を描いたもので、6枚のパネルが一揃いとなった6曲屏風。

図156　屏風の隅飾り金具。
図157　屏風の収納箱。屏風はたたんで絹の袋に入れてから、箱に収納される。
図158　屏風の足支え、陶製。
図159　風炉先屏風（ふろさきびょうぶ）、茶の湯を沸かす釜の前に置いて、風から風炉を守るためのもの。
図160　小型の陶製の衝立（ついたて）、墨をするときに硯の前に置いて畳を汚さないようにするためのもの。
図161　衝立。
図162　竹の簾（すだれ）、竹の節をＺ形に置いたり（A）、薄い竹の下に正方形の切れ目を入れたりする（B）。
図163　竹の簾（すだれ）、図162のようにつくると、部屋の陰影によってこのようなデザインがあらわれてくる。
図164　几帳（きちょう）、漆を塗った台に2本の柱を立てて横木を渡して、そこに薄い布（帳）をかけたもの。
図165　飾りのついた、竹製の暖簾（のれん）。
図166　布を裂いたかたちの暖簾。

〈台所・階段 など〉
図167　古い農家の台所、武蔵・青山〔埼玉県熊谷市〕。富裕な自作農家の典型的な台所で、築200年近いという。手前の大きな木枠は井戸で、ロープの付いた滑車が下がっている。奥の2人の女性は、脚の付いた漆塗りの御膳に皿を並べて、夕食の準備をしている。左奥の竈（かまど）には飯を炊いているであろう釜が二つ、湯気を立てている。竈のそばには七輪（図171参照）も見える。床は厚い板張りで、よく磨かれている。
図168　図167の台所の竈（かまど）。通常、竈は粘土や泥に割れたタイルなどを練り込み、漆喰（しっくい）を塗って外側を黒くする。
図169　煙突が付いた竈、東京・今戸。煙を出すためのブリキのフードが付いているが、これは現代的な工夫であろう。
図170　都市の住宅の台所、東京。ここの竈は隅に吸い込み口のあるがっしりとした石製のもので、そのそばに炭の火消し壺や七輪が見える。板敷きの床を降りたところに流しがあり、その上の吊り棚には釜や桶などが置かれている。
図171　七輪（しちりん）。炭を効率よく使え、湯を沸かしたりするのに便利である。
図172　竹筒の整理棚と包丁入れ。どこの家の台所にもたいがいこれがある（図167・170参照）。
図173　自在（じざい）。炉の上に吊るされて、高さを自由に調整できることから、この名がある。自在鉤（じざいかぎ）ともいう。図は、農家にある簡単な鉄瓶吊るしで、竹製。
図174　農家の囲炉裏（いろり）。部屋の中央に炉が切ってあり、その上の天井から鎖で鉄瓶を吊るしている。また、太い藁束に魚を串刺しにしていぶしてもいる。北国や農村でよく見られる台所の様子。

図175　高級な囲炉裏。手前の四角い箱は銅製で、酒を温めるもの。
図176　高さを調節できる鉄瓶吊るし。あまり見かけることはない、珍しいもの。
図177　台所の箱段（はこだん）。物入れ・引出し・階段などが一体になっている。階段簞笥（たんす）ともいう。下の物入れには、燭台（しょくだい）や行灯（あんどん）が入っている（図205‐207参照）
図178　階段の手すり。皇居の庭に新しく造られた建物に、簡素だが粋な階段と手すりが付けられていた。
図179　縁側の階段。2枚の側板の柄穴（ほぞあな）に厚板を嵌め込んで段にしている。

〈風呂場・洗面所 など〉
図180　横に焚口がある浴槽（風呂桶）。
図181　内側に管がある浴槽。
図182　外部に焚口がある広い浴槽の断面図。
図183　焚口が浴槽の外側にあるタイプ。
図184　底が鉄でできた浴槽、五右衛門風呂と呼ばれる。底の鉄底を直に温めるので、やけどしないように板を沈めてその上に乗って入浴する。
図185　田舎の宿屋の洗面所。底の浅い木の箱に水桶と銅製の洗面器が入っていて、縁側や廊下の隅に置かれている。
図186　個人住宅の洗面所。廊下の端などによく見られるもので、明るく、簡素だがこぎれいで良い。水の入った立派な壺、銅製の洗面器、きれいな柄杓（ひしゃく）、ちょっと風変わりな手拭い掛け。
図187　日本の書物から写した洗面所。片側に低い衝立（ついたて）があり、左側の台に載った水甕（みずがめ）には柄杓、右側の流しの底は竿竹でできていて流した水は下の溝に流れ込む。正面の壁には行灯（あんどん）、右の壁には手拭いが掛かっている。
図188‐192　いろいろな手拭い掛け。

〈枕・火鉢・たばこ盆〉
図193　ふだんよく使われる枕。木の箱の上にそば殻を詰めた筒状のクッションと枕紙を糸でくくり付けている。
図194　枕を使っているときの姿勢。
図195　掘炬燵（ほりごたつ）。
図196　肘休め（ひじやすめ）のための円いクッション。
図197　一般的な木製の火鉢。銅で裏打ちした木箱に黒い素焼きの丸壺を入れたもの。持ち運びしやすいように指を入れる穴があいている。
図198　堅い木材をくりぬいた火鉢。内側は銅で、塗りも厚い。
図199　ぶ厚い部屋着にくるまって火鉢で暖を取っている。
図200　会合のときの火鉢の置き方。
図201　たばこ盆。小型の火鉢のようなもので、喫煙者のための道具であり、中には炭の入った小さな壺と竹筒が入っている。竹筒は痰壺（たんつぼ）である。

図 202　樫（かし）の木の節のあるくぼみを利用した、たばこ盆。
図 203　持ち運びしやすいように工夫された、たばこ盆。
図 204　おこした炭を運ぶときに使う、底の浅い鉄製の片手鍋、台十能（だいじゅうのう）。

〈燭台・行灯・神棚〉
図 205　鉄製の燭台（しょくだい）、手燭。図 177 に一般的な形の燭台が見られる。
図 206　一般的な置き行灯（あんどん）。
図 207　置き行灯。覆いがいろいろな方向に開き、中に油入れの皿を置く棚が付いている。
図 208　漆塗りの灯明台（とうみょうだい）、古い絵本から模写。
図 209　壁に取り付けられた、珍しい型の行灯
図 210　鉄製で、吊るすタイプの灯明台。
図 211　陶器製の灯明台（織部焼）。
図 212　陶器製の灯明台（伊賀焼）。
図 213　陶器製の燭台（尾張焼）。
図 214　固定された提灯の街灯。
図 215　家の社（やしろ）。
図 216　個人の家にあるツバメの巣。

〈かわや〉
図 217　ふつうよく見られるかわやの内部。
図 218　宿屋のかわや、日光・鉢石村〔栃木県日光市〕。手前の縁側から右に曲がると、自然木で縁取りされた狭い廊下になり、かわやへと導かれる。入口の壁はねじれたブドウの木で縁取られていて、その奥に開き戸があるが、日本の家で開き戸があるのはここぐらいである。屋根は柿葺きで、外壁に沿って垣根があり、木や花が植えられている。水桶と洗面器を置く 4 本足の台が見えるが、これは外国人客のためのもので、手水鉢（ちょうずばち）が置かれるのが普通である。
図 219　東京・浅草の商家のかわや。色の異なるいろいろな木をちりばめたデザインの戸がある。
図 220　図 219 の内部。

〈玄　関〉
図 221　住まいの表玄関、図 36・37 の家の出入口で、ここは武士の家だが、普通の家の玄関の典型といえる。
図 222　上流階級の家の玄関と式台の平面図。手前の入口から障子までの空間は、母屋から飛び出している。
図 223　古い家の狭い玄関にあった下駄箱のスケッチ、東京・上野。
図 224　玄関の提灯棚、提灯には家紋や家の名前が書かれている。
図 225　商家の、引戸が付いた格子戸（こうしど）。引戸を開けて、少し高い敷居をま

たいで、土間と呼ばれる床に足を踏み入れる。

〈縁　側〉
図226　縁側の床、床板の張り方。縁側が折れ曲がるところで、双方の厚板の端が斜めに切られる（A）か、方形に接する（B）。この床板には、角を深く面取りしたり、丸くそいだ厚板を使う場合も見られる（C）。縁側にかんしては、図37・48・49・50・95、また平面図（図97・98）や断面図（図103）を参照。

図227　京都の古い民家の縁側。幅広い屋根を支える柱、庇（ひさし）と呼ばれる補助的な屋根、一部開け放たれた障子、などの興味深い情景が描かれている。

図228　2階縁側（バルコニー・ベランダ）の手すり（欄干）の様子。Aの部分が取りはずしできて、ごみなどを掃き出せるようになっている。

図229　打抜き細工のパネルが付けられた、2階縁側の手すり、松島。

図230　2階縁側の手すり。かたどって細工したパネルを赤松の丸棒で縁取ったものが取り付けられている。

図231　欄干に細い竹を使って繊細な感じを出している、2階縁側の手すり。

図232　がんじょうなつくりの2階縁側の手すり。柱の頭は金属で作られ、上の横木にも一定間隔で金属板が打ち付けられている。

〈雨　戸〉
図233　雨戸の錠、施錠していない状態。
図234　雨戸の錠、施錠している状態。
図235　雨戸の鋲（びょう、knob）。古い家では雨戸の敷居の外側に鉄製の鋲が打ち込まれている。雨戸が浮き上がって敷居から外れないための工夫であるが、めったに見受けられない。

図236　雨戸を直角に曲げるための仕組み（コーナー・ローラー）。小さな鉄のローラーが角に固定されていて、雨戸が角までくると押し出されて敷居の溝を離れるが、そこで90度回転して直行する溝に入るようになっている。

図237　回転する戸袋と手水鉢（ちょうずばち）のある縁側。住宅の外壁部分にある戸袋は光をさえぎることにもなるので、雨戸をしまった後に縁側と直角になるように戸袋を回転させて、玄関のほうの壁などにくっつける。

〈手水鉢〉
図238　いちばん単純な手水鉢（ちょうずばち）。木製のバケツを竹で吊り下げたもので、その竹は縁側の軒先にぶらさがり、竹の柄杓（ひしゃく）が添えられる。たいてい手ぬぐい掛けがそばにある。図218参照。

図239　難破船の舵柱で作られたという、手水鉢。
図240　円筒形の石をくりぬいた、手水鉢。
図241　手水鉢と庇縁（ひさしえん）。縁側の端から突き出た小さな台（庇縁）の先に手水鉢が置かれている。ここで手を洗う様子は、図227参照。

〈門〉

図242　屋敷の門、東京・九段。がんじょうでどっしりとした構造の建物についている。格子で囲われた窓は門番用で、ここから人の出入りを監視する。門の前には幅の狭い、深い堀があり、石橋が渡されている。

図243　内側から見た都市の上流階級の住宅の門。左右の本柱は控え柱と添え木で補強され、両開きの戸はがんじょうな木のかんぬきで渡し込まれている。門には小さな引戸が付いていて、通常はここから出入りする。この小さなくぐり戸を出入りすると、呼び鈴が鳴ったり、ひもに結んであるものが音を立てる仕掛けになっている（図244参照）ことが多い。

図244　門の鳴子。

図245　門の小さな引戸のかんぬき。

図246　家と庭を囲む背の高い木の塀につくられた簡素な門、東京・上野。

図247　都市の邸宅の門。戸の表面薄く剝いだ杉皮を編んだものを使い、上部には木格子がはめこまれている。

図248　東京近郊の門。2本の門柱は樹皮を剝いだだけの自然木で、上に載っている横木は鳥居のような反りをもっている。門の両側の板塀や竹塀、門の前に置かれた不規則な形の敷石とそれを取り囲む玉石、など、均整のとれた美しさとデザインの清楚さに驚かされる。

図249　変わった趣味の門。頂部の横木には太くて曲がった丸太が使われている。

図250　田舎風の門、東京郊外および南日本で典型的な門。

図251　皇居の広い庭で見た、田舎風の門。2本の丸太が門柱となり、垣根は三本一組の太い竹で作られている。

図252　図251と同じ場所で見かけた、田舎風の庭の戸。丸い門柱に細い板を編みこんだようなかろやかな戸。塀は葦で作られている。

図253　風変わりな、庭の門。この門の向こうには別の庭があり、門の向こうの右手の建物は茶室で、左上の軒に下がる木魚は、叩いて音を出し、客室から奥の茶室へ客を呼び出すためのもの。

〈塀・垣〉

図254　ふつうの木製の塀（へい）。

図255　杭（くい）を使った塀。

図256　竹を使ったすばらしい塀。横木が竹で塀に織り込まれたようになっている。

図257　ひじょうに堅固で耐久性のある塀、箱根〔神奈川県〕。

図258　田舎風の庭にある、装飾性の強い塀。下の方は小枝の束と細長い横木で押さえ、上の方は赤松の小枝を使った格子に細いつるがはめこまれている。

図259　袖垣（そでがき）、円筒状に束ねられた藺草（いぐさ）を黒い繊維の根で結びつけている。

図260　図259と似たタイプの袖垣。円筒状の柴と藺草の束が2本ずつ交互に並んで結び付けられている。

図261　変わった型の袖垣。茶色の藺草の束が幅いっぱいに垂れ下がり、頂部には葦の太い束が載せられ、黒いシュロ縄で縛りつけられている。
図262　塀に付けられた格子窓。

〈灯籠 など〉
図263　庭に置かれた石製の銘板。
図264　東京の石灯籠（いしどうろう）。
図265　宮島の境内にあった石灯籠。
図266　武蔵・白子村〔埼玉県和光市〕の石灯籠。
図267　宇都宮の石灯籠。

〈庭の橋〉
図268　石の渡し橋。
図269　石橋。
図270　庭の小川と石橋。

〈東屋・窓・路地〉
図271　東京のある住宅の庭にある東屋（あずまや）。
図272　皇居御苑の一隅にある東屋。
図273　ひょうたんの形をした、東屋の明り窓、神戸〔兵庫県〕。
図274　山の形に竹格子が入った、東屋の明り窓、岡崎〔愛知県〕。
図275　庭の路地の敷石のパターン、『築山庭造伝』から写す。図283・284も参照。

〈植木鉢・盆栽 など〉
図276　古い難破船の破片を利用して作られた水盤。
図277　古い舟板材で作られた大きな植木鉢。
図278　盆栽のスモモ。
図279　盆栽の松。
図280　不思議な形の松の木。
図281　盆栽の松。
図282　冬に植木を藁でおおう、雪囲い。

〈庭の景色 など〉
図283　住まいへのアプローチ（『築山庭造伝』より）。
図284　仏教寺院の住職の小庭（『築山庭造伝』より）。
図285　商家の庭（『築山庭造伝』より）。
図286　大名の庭（『築山庭造伝』より）。

〈井戸・給水 など〉
図287　井桁（いげた）の古い形態。
図288　東京の個人住宅の石造井桁。
図289　木製の釣瓶（つるべ）井戸。
図290　ツタに覆われた木の幹をそのまま利用した、釣瓶井戸。
図291　貯水施設、安芸・宮島〔広島県〕。山の泉から竹のパイプで水を引いてきて、自然岩を積み上げた台座の上に置かれた底の浅い貯水槽に水を貯める。貯水槽の横にはいくつもの穴があいていて、そこから水は、頭部に箱や桶を持つ竹筒に流れ、さらに地下に敷設されている竹筒に流れて、下流にある村の家々に届けられる。
図292　筧（かけひ、懸け樋）、宮島の水道システム。
図293　加賀屋敷の井戸、東京。

〈花〉
図294　竹製の花生け。
図295　籠細工（かございく）の花生け。
図296　花器を載せる張出し棚。
図297　手桶を組合せた独創的な花器。

〈いろいろな物〉
図298　支えの付いた額縁。
図299　柱隠し。
図300　文机（ふづくえ）。
図301　桶と箒が載った、屋根の上の台。
図302　葛（つづら）、運搬用の箱。

〈そのほかの家〉
図303　マレーの家、シンガポール近郊。
図304　屋根の棟、安南・チョロン〔ヴェトナム南部〕。
図305　寝床が見えるマレーの住宅内部、シンガポール。
図306　アイヌの家、蝦夷〔北海道〕。
図307　アイヌの家、蝦夷〔北海道〕。

LIST OF ILLUSTRATIONS.

VIEWS OF CITY AND VILLAGE.

FIG. 1. A VIEW IN TOKIO, SHOWING SHOPS AND HOUSES. (COPIED FROM A PHOTOGRAPH.)
" 2. A VIEW IN TOKIO, SHOWING TEMPLES AND GARDENS. (COPIED FROM A PHOTOGRAPH.)
" 3. VIEW OF ENOSHIMA. (COPIED FROM A PHOTOGRAPH.)

HOUSE CONSTRUCTION.

FIG. 4. SIDE-FRAMING
" 5. POUNDING DOWN FOUNDATION STONES
" 6. FOUNDATION STONE
" 7. SECTION OF FRAMING
" 8. FRAMING
" 9. END-FRAMING OF LARGE BUILDING
" 10. ROOF-FRAME OF LARGE BUILDING
" 11. ROOF-FRAMING OF KURA
" 12. FRAMING OF AN ORDINARY TWO-STORIED HOUSE. (FROM A JAPANESE DRAWING)
" 13. OUTSIDE BRACES
" 14. OUTSIDE BRACE
" 15. ORNAMENTAL BRACE
" 16. METHOD OF CUTTING TIMBER FOR HOUSE-FINISH
" 17. SECTION OF POST GROOVED FOR PARTITION
" 18. BUNDLE OF BOARDS
" 19. SECTION OF CEILING
" 20. CEILING-RAFTERS SUPPORTED TEMPORARILY
" 21. METHOD OF SUSPENDING CEILING AS SEEN FROM ABOVE
" 22. CEILING-BOARD WEIGHTED WITH STONES
" 23. CEILING-BOARD IN CLOSET

Fig. 24. Method of removing Boards from Bundle to preserve Uniformity of Grain
" 25. Arrangement of Square Tiles on Side of House

CARPENTERS' TOOLS, ETC.

Fig. 26. A Japanese Carpenter's Vise
" 27. Carpenter's Tools in Common Use
" 28. A Japanese Nail-basket
" 29. A Carpenter's Marking-brush made of Wood
" 30. The Sumi-tsubo
" 31. The Japanese Plumb-line
" 32. Ancient Carpenter (Copied from an Old Painting)

CITY AND COUNTRY HOUSES.

Fig. 33. Street in Kanda Ku, Tokio
" 34. Street in Kanda Ku, Tokio
" 35. Block of Cheap Tenements in Tokio
" 36. Street View of Dwelling in Tokio
" 37. View of Dwelling from Garden, in Tokio
" 38. Dwelling near Kudan, Tokio
" 39. Country Inn in Rikuzen
" 40. Country Inn in Rikuzen
" 41. House near Mororan, Yezo
" 42. Bay-window, Village of Odzuka, Rikuzen
" 43. Three-storied House in Rikuchiu
" 44. Street in the Suburbs of Morioka
" 45. Old Farm-house in Kabutoyama
" 46. Entrance to Court-yard of Old House in Kioto
" 47. Old House in Kioto. Court-yard View
" 48. Old House in Kioto. Garden View
" 49. House in Tokio
" 50. View from Second Story of Dwelling in Imado, Tokio
" 51. Old Inn in Mishima, Suruga
" 52. Village Street in Nagaike, Yamashiro
" 53. Shore of Ōsumi
" 54. Farmers' Houses in Mototarumidsu, Ōsumi
" 55. Fishermen's Huts in Hakodate
" 56. Fishermen's Houses at Enoshima
" 57. Kura in Tokio
" 58. Kura, or Fire-proof Buildings in Tokio (From Sketch by S. Koyama)
" 59. Old House in Hakodate

SHINGLED ROOFS, ETC.

Fig. 60. Hisashi
" 61. Bunch of Shingles, Nails, and Hammer
" 62. Shingler's Hand
" 63. Bamboo Strips on Shingle-roof
" 64. Roof with Shingles partly laid
" 65. Ridge of Shingle-roof in Musashi
" 66. Water-conductor

TILED ROOFS, ETC.

Fig. 67. Ridge of Tiled Roof
" 68. Ornamental Coping of Tiles
" 69. Ornamental Coping of Tiles
" 70. Ornamental Coping of Tiles
" 71. Eaves of Tiled Roof
" 72. Nagasaki Tiled Roof
" 73. Hon-gawara, or True Tile
" 74. Yedo-gawara, or Yedo-tile Eaves
" 75. French-tile Eaves
" 76. Iwami Tile for Ridge
" 77. Stone Roof

THATCHED ROOFS, ETC.

Fig. 78. Thatch and Thatchers' Implements
" 79. End of Roof in Fujita, Iwaki
" 80. Tiled Ridge of Thatched Roof in Iwaki
" 81. Tiled Ridge of Thatched Roof in Musashi
" 82. Bamboo Ridge of Thatched Roof in Musashi
" 83. Thatched Roof, near Tokio
" 84. Thatched Roof, near Tokio. (From Photograph taken by Percival Lowell, Esq.)
" 85. Ridge of Thatched Roof at Kabutoyama, Musashi
" 86. Crest of Thatched Roof in Omi
" 87. Tile and Bamboo Ridge of Thatched Roof, Takatsuki, Setsu
" 88. Crest of Thatched Roof in Mikawa
" 89. Crest of Thatched Roof in Kioto
" 90. Crest of Thatched Roof in Mikawa
" 91. Crest of Thatched Roof in Kii
" 92. Thatched Roof in Yamato

Fig. 93. Crest of Thatched Roof in Tōtōmi
" 94. Crest of Thatched Roof in Ise.
" 95. Paved space under Eaves of Thatched Roof

INTERIORS, PLANS, MATS, SLIDING SCREENS, ETC.

Fig. 96. Guest-room at Hachi-ishi
" 97. Plan of Dwelling-house in Tokio
" 98. Plan of Dwelling-house in Tokio
" 99. Plan of a Portion of a Daimio's Residence
" 100. Mat
" 101. Arrangement of Mats in different-sized Rooms
" 102. Attitude of Woman in Sitting
" 103. Section through Verandah and Guest-room
" 104. Reed-screen
" 105. Sliding Panel
" 106. Hikite
" 107. Hikite
" 108. Hikite
" 109. Hikite
" 110. Hikite with Cord
" 111. Straightening Shōji-frame
" 112. Shōji with Ornamental Frame.
" 113. Portion of Toko-bashira
" 114–117. Ornamental-headed Nails
" 118. Shelves contrasted with Conventional Drawing of Mist, or Clouds

INTERIORS SHOWING TOKONOMA AND CHIGAI-DANA.

Fig. 119. Guest-room
" 120. Guest-room, with Recesses in Corner
" 121. Guest-room, showing Circular Window
" 122. Guest-room, showing Writing-place
" 123. Guest-room, with wide Tokonoma
" 124. Small Guest-room
" 125. Guest-room of Dwelling in Tokio
" 126. Guest-room in Kiyomidzu, Kioto
" 127. Guest-room of Dwelling in Tokio
" 128. Guest-room of a Country House
" 129. Corner of Guest-room

TEA-ROOMS.

Fig. 130. Tea-room in Nan-en-ji Temple, Kioto
" 131. Tea-room in Fujimi Pottery, Nagoya
" 132. Tea-room in Miyajima
" 133. Kitchen for Tea-utensils
" 134. Tea-room in Imado, Tokio
" 135. Corner of Tea-room shown in Fig. 134

KURA INTERIORS, DOORS, ETC.

Fig. 136. Room in Second Story of Old Building in Kawagoye, Musashi
" 137. Room in Kura fitted up as a Library, Tokio
" 138. Framework for Draping Room in Kura. (Copied from a Japanese Work)
" 139. Space between Dwelling and Kura, roofed over and utilized as a Kitchen in Tokio
" 140. Doorway of an old Kura in Kioto
" 141. Key to Kura, and Bunch of Keys
" 142. Padlock to Kura

CEILING, RAMMA, WINDOWS.

Fig. 143. Panelled Ceiling
" 144. Ramma in Hakóne Village
" 145. Bamboo Ramma
" 146. Porcelain Ramma in Tokio
" 147. Ramma of Bamboo and Perforated Panel
" 148. Carved-wood Ramma in Gojio Village, Yamato
" 149. Carved-wood Ramma in Town of Yatsushiro, Higo
" 150. Ramma, composed of two Thin Boards, in Nagoya, Owari
" 151. Shōji for Window
" 152. Shōji-frame for Window
" 153. Shōji-frame for Window
" 154. Window

PORTABLE SCREENS, CURTAINS, ETC.

Fig. 155. Biyō-bu, or Folding Screen
" 156. Wrought metallic mounting of Screen Frame
" 157. Screen-box
" 158. Foot-weight for Screen

Fig. 159. Furosaki biyō-bu
" 160. Model of Tsui-tate in Pottery
" 161. Tsui-tate
" 162. Bamboo Curtains
" 163. Bamboo Curtain
" 164. Curtain-screen
" 165. Fringed Curtain
" 166. Slashed Curtain

KITCHENS, STAIRWAYS, ETC.

Fig. 167. Kitchen in old Farmhouse at Kabutoyama
" 168. Kitchen Range
" 169. Kitchen Range with Smoke-conductor
" 170. Kitchen in City House
" 171. Braziers
" 172. Bamboo Rack and Knife-case
" 173. Ji-zai
" 174. Fireplace in Country House
" 175. The best Fireplace
" 176. An Adjustable Device for supporting a Kettle
" 177. Kitchen Closet, Drawers, Cupboard, and Stairs combined
" 178. Stair-rail
" 179. Steps to Verandah

BATHING CONVENIENCES.

Fig. 180. Bath-tub, with Side Oven
" 181. Bath-tub, with Inside Flue
" 182. Bath-tub in Section, with Oven outside the Room
" 183. Bath-tub, with outside Heating-chamber
" 184. Bath-tub, with Iron Base
" 185. Lavatory in Country Inn
" 186. Lavatory in Private House
" 187. Lavatory copied from Japanese Book
" 188-192. Forms of Towel-racks

PILLOWS, HIBACHI, AND TABAKO-BON.

Fig. 193. Forms of Pillow in common use
" 194. Showing position of Head in resting on Pillow
" 195. Heating Arrangement in Floor

FIG. 196. ELBOW-REST
" 197. COMMON HIBACHI
" 198. HIBACHI
" 199. HIBACHI
" 200. HIBACHI ARRANGED FOR COMPANY
" 201. TABAKO-BON
" 202. TABAKO-BON
" 203. TABAKO-BON
" 204. PAN FOR HOLDING BURNING CHARCOAL

CANDLESTICKS, LAMPS, SHRINES, ETC.

FIG. 205. IRON CANDLESTICK
" 206. LAMP
" 207. LAMP
" 208. LAMP AND LACQUERED STAND. (COPIED FROM A JAPANESE WORK.)
" 209. WALL-LAMP
" 210. LAMP
" 211. POTTERY LAMP
" 212. POTTERY LAMP
" 213. POTTERY CANDLESTICK
" 214. FIXED STREET-LANTERN
" 215. HOUSEHOLD SHRINE
" 216. SWALLOWS' NESTS IN PRIVATE HOUSE

PRIVIES.

FIG. 217. INTERIOR OF PRIVY
" 218. PRIVY OF INN IN HACHI-ISHI VILLAGE, NIKKO
" 219. PRIVY CONNECTED WITH A MERCHANT'S HOUSE IN ASAKUSA
" 220. INTERIOR OF A PRIVY IN ASAKUSA

ENTRANCE AND HALL.

FIG. 221. MAIN ENTRANCE TO HOUSE
" 222. PLAN OF VESTIBULE AND HALL
" 223. SHOE-CLOSET
" 224. LANTERN-SHELF IN HALL
" 225. GRATED ENTRANCE WITH SLIDING DOOR

VERANDAH AND BALCONY.

FIG. 226. VERANDAH FLOOR
" 227. VERANDAH OF AN OLD KIOTO HOUSE

Fig. 228. Balcony Rail
" 229. Balcony Rail and Perforated Panels
" 230. Balcony Rail
" 231. Balcony Rail
" 232. Balcony Rail

AMADO.

Fig. 233. Rain-door Lock unbolted
" 234. Rain-door Lock bolted
" 235. Knob for Rain-door
" 236. Corner-roller for Rain-door
" 237. Verandah showing Swinging Closet for Rain-doors and also Chōdzu-bachi

CHŌDZU-BACHI.

Fig. 238. Chōdzu-bachi
" 239. Chōdzu-bachi
" 240. Chōdzu-bachi
" 241. Chōdzu-bachi and Hisashi-yen

GATEWAYS.

Fig. 242. Gateway in Yashiki Building
" 243. Gateway of City House from within
" 244. Gate-rattle
" 245. Bolt for little Sliding Door in Gateway
" 246. Gateway to City Residence
" 247. Gateway to City Residence
" 248. Gateway near Tokio
" 249. Gateway
" 250. Rustic Gateway
" 251. Rustic Gateway
" 252. Rustic Garden Gate
" 253. Garden Gateway

FENCES.

Fig. 254. Ordinary Wooden Fence
" 255. Stake Fence
" 256. Bamboo Fence
" 257. Fence in Hakōne Village

Fig. 258. Rustic Garden-fence
" 259. Sode-gaki
" 260. Sode-gaki
" 261. Sode-gaki
" 262. Barred Opening in Fence

STONE LANTERNS, ETC.

Fig. 263. Garden Tablet
" 264. Ishi-dōrō in Tokio
" 265. Ishi-dōrō in Miyajima
" 266. Ishi-dōrō in Shirako, Musashi
" 267. Ishi-dōrō in Utsunomiya

GARDEN BRIDGES.

Fig. 268. Stone Foot-bridge
" 269. Stone Foot-bridge
" 270. Garden Brook and Foot-bridge

SUMMER-HOUSES, WINDOWS, AND PATHS.

Fig. 271. Summer-house in Private Garden, Tokio
" 272. Summer-house in Imperial Garden, Tokio
" 273. Rustic Opening in Summer-house, Kobe
" 274. Rustic Opening in Summer-house, Okazaki
" 275. Various Forms of Garden Paths

FLOWER-POTS, DWARF-TREES, ETC.

Fig. 276. Wooden Trough for Plants
" 277. Plant-pot of old Plank
" 278. Dwarf Plum
" 279. Dwarf Pine
" 280 Curiously trained Pine-tree
" 281. Dwarfed Pine
" 282. Shrubs wrapped in Straw for Winter

GARDEN VIEWS.

Fig. 283. Showing Approaches to House. (Reproduced from "Chikusan Teizoden," a Japanese Work.)
" 284. Little Garden belonging to the Priests of a Buddhist Temple. (Reproduced from "Chikusan Teizoden," a Japanese Work.)

Fig. 285. Garden of a Merchant. (Reproduced from "Chikusan Teizo-
          den," a Japanese Work.)
 "   286. Garden of a Daimio. (Reproduced from "Chikusan Teizoden,"
          a Japanese Work.)

WELLS AND WATER-SUPPLY.

Fig. 287. Ancient Form of Well-curb
 "   288. Stone Well-curb in Private Garden in Tokio
 "   289. Wooden Well-frame
 "   290. Rustic Well-frame
 "   291. Aqueduct Reservoir at Miyajima, Aki
 "   292. Aqueducts at Miyajima, Aki
 "   293. Well in Kaga Yashiki, Tokio

FLOWERS.

Fig. 294. Hanging Flower-holder of Bamboo
 "   295. Hanging Flower-holder of Basket-work
 "   296. Cheap Bracket for Flower-pots
 "   297. Curious Combination of Buckets for Flowers

MISCELLANEOUS.

Fig. 298. Framed Picture, with Supports
 "   299. Hashira-kakushi
 "   300. Writing-desk
 "   301. Staging on House-roof, with bucket and brush
 "   302. Box for Transporting Articles

OTHER HOUSES.

Fig. 303. Malay House near Singapore
 "   304. Ridge of Roof in Cholon, Anam
 "   305. Interior of Malay House, showing Bed-place. Singapore
 "   306. Aino House, Yezo
 "   307. Aino House, Yezo

GLOSSARY.

In the following list of Japanese words used in this work an opportunity is given to correct a number of mistakes which crept into, or rather walked boldly into, the text. The author lays no claim to a knowledge of the Japanese language beyond what any foreigner might naturally acquire in being thrown among the people for some time. As far as possible he has followed Hepburn's Japanese Dictionary for orthography and definition, and Brunton's Map of Japan for geographical names. Brunton's map, as well as that published by Rein, spells Settsu with one *t*. For the sake of uniformity I have followed this spelling in the text, though it is contrary to the best authorities. It may be added that Ōshiu and Tōtōmi should be printed with a long accent over each *o*.

The words Samurai, Daimio, Kioto, Tokio, and several others, are now so commonly seen in the periodical literature of our country that this form of spelling for these words has been retained. For rules concerning the pronunciation of Japanese words the reader is referred to the Introduction in Hepburn's Dictionary.

Agari-ba	The floor for standing upon in coming out of the bath.
Age-yen	A platform that can be raised or lowered.
Amado	Rain-door. The outside sliding doors by which the house is closed at night.
Andon	A lamp.
Asagao	A colloquial name for a porcelain urinal, from its resemblance to the flower of the morning-glory.
Benjo	Privy. Place for business.
Biwa	A lute with four strings.
Biyō-bu	A folding screen.
Cha-dokoro	Tea-place.
Cha-ire	Tea-jar; literally, "tea-put in."
Cha-no-yu	A tea-party.
Chigai-dana	A shelf, one half of which is on a different plane from the other.

Chōdzu-ba . . .	Privy; literally, "hand water-place."
Chōdzu-bachi .	A convenience near the privy for washing the hands.
Chū-nuri . . .	Middle layer of plaster.
Dai-jū-no . . .	A pan for holding burning charcoal, used in replenishing the hibachi.
Daiku	A carpenter.
Daimio	A feudal lord.
Dodai	The foundation-sill of a house.
Dodai-ishi . . .	Foundation stone.
Do-ma	Earth-space. A small unfloored court at the entrance of the house.
Fukuro-dana . .	Cupboard; literally, "pouch-shelf."
Fumi-ishi . . .	Stepping-stone.
Furo	A small culinary furnace, also a bath-tub.
Furosaki biyō-bu .	A two-fold screen placed in front of the furo.
Fusuma	A sliding screen between rooms.
Fu-tai	The bands which hang down in front of a kake-mono; literally, "wind-band."
Futon	A quilted bed-cover.
Ge-dan	Lower step.
Genka	The porch at the entrance of a house.
Geta	Wooden clogs.
Goyemon buro .	A form of bath-tub.
Habakari . . .	Privy.
Hagi	A kind of rush.
Hashira	A post.
Hashira kakushi .	A long narrow picture to hang on post in room; literally, "post-hide."
Hibachi	A brazier for holding hot coals for warming the apartments.
Hibashi	Metal tongs.
Hikite	A recessed catch in a screen for sliding it back and forth.
Hi-no-ki . . .	A species of pine.
Hisashi	A small roof projecting over a door or window.
Hon-gawara . .	True tile.

Ichi-yo-dana	A kind of shelf.
Iri-kawa	The space between the verandah and room.
Ishi-dōrō	A stone lantern.
Ji-bukuro	Cupboard.
Jin-dai-sugi	"Cedar of God's age."
Jinrikisha	A two-wheeled vehicle drawn by a man.
Ji-zai	A hook used for hanging pots over the fire.
Jō-dan	Upper step. Raised floor in house.
Kago	Sedan chair.
Kaikōsha	Name of a private school of architecture.
Kake-mono	Hanging picture.
Kaki	Fence.
Kamado	Kitchen range.
Kami-dana	A shelf in the house for Shin-tō shrine.
Kami-no-ma	Higher room.
Kamoi	Lintel.
Kara-kami	Sliding screen between rooms.
Kawarake	Unglazed earthen ware.
Kaya	A kind of grass used for thatch.
Kaya	Mosquito netting.
Kazari-kugi	Ornamental headed nails.
Kaze-obi	The bands which hang down in front of the kake-mono; literally, "wind-band."
Keshō-no-ma	Toilet-room.
Keyaki	A kind of hard wood.
Kō-ka	Privy; literally, "back frame."
Koshi-bari	A kind of paper used for a dado.
Kuguri-do	A small, low door in a gate.
Kura	A fire-proof store-house.
Kuro-moji-gaki	A kind of ornamental fence.
Ma-bashira	Middle post.
Mado	Window.
Ma-gaki	A fence made of bamboo.
Magari-gane	A carpenter's iron square.
Maki-mono	Pictures that are kept rolled up, not hung.

Maki-mono-dana .	Shelf for maki-mono.
Makura	Pillow.
Miki-dokkuri . .	Bottle for offering wine to gods.
Mochi	A kind of bread made of glutinous rice.
Mon	Badge, or crest.
Mune	Ridge of roof.
Naka-tsubo . .	Middle space.
Nan-do	Store-room. Pantry.
Neda-maruta . .	Cross-beams to support floor.
Nedzumi-bashira	Cross-beam at end of building; literally, "rat-post."
Nikai-bari . . .	Horizontal beam to support second-story floor.
Noren	Curtain. Hanging screen.
Nuki	A stick passed through mortised holes to bind together upright posts.
Nuri-yen . . .	A verandah unprotected by amado.
Ochi-yen . . .	A low platform.
Oshi-ire	Closet; literally, "push, put in."
Otoshi-kake . .	Hanging partition.
Ramma	Open ornamental work over the screens which form the partitions in the house.
Ro	Hearth, or fire-place, in the floor.
Rō-ka	Corridor. Covered way.
Sake	Fermented liquor brewed from rice.
Samisen . . .	A guitar with three strings.
Samisen-tsugi . .	A peculiar splice for joining timber.
Samurai . . .	Military class privileged to wear two swords.
Sashi-mono-ya .	Cabinet-maker.
Setsu-in . . .	Privy; literally, "snow-hide."
Shaku	A wooden tablet formerly carried by nobles when in the presence of the Emperor.
Shaku	A measure of ten inches. Japanese foot.
Shichirin . . .	A brazier for cooking purposes.
Shikii	The lower grooved beam in which the door or screens slide.
Shin-tō	The primitive religion of Japan.

Shita-nuri . . .	The first layer of plaster.
Shō-ji	The outside door-sash covered with thin paper.
Sode-gaki . . .	A small ornamental fence adjoining a house.
Sudare	A shade made of split bamboo or reeds.
Sugi	Cedar.
Sumi-sashi . . .	A marking-brush made of wood.
Sumi-tsubo . .	An ink-pot used by carpenters in lieu of the chalk-line.
Sūn	One tenth of a Japanese foot.
Sunoko	A platform made of bamboo.
Tabako-bon . .	A box or tray in which fire and smoking utensils are kept.
Tamari-no-ma . .	Anteroom.
Tansu	Bureau.
Taruki	A rafter of the roof.
Tatami	A floor-mat.
Ten-jō	Ceiling.
Te-shoku . . .	Hand-lamp.
To-bukuro . . .	A closet in which outside doors are stowed away.
Tokkuri	A bottle.
To-ko	The floor of the tokonoma.
Toko-bashira . .	The post dividing the two bays or recesses in the guest-room.
Tokonoma . . .	A bay, or recess, where a picture is hung.
Tori-i	A portal, or structure of stone or wood, erected in front of a Shin-tō temple.
Tsubo	An area of six feet square.
Tsugi-no-ma . .	Second room.
Tsui-tate . . .	A screen of one leaf set in a frame.
Tsume-sho . . .	A servant's waiting-room.
Usukasumi-dana .	A name for shelf; literally, "thin mist-shelf."
Uwa-nuri . . .	The last layer of plaster.
Watari	A passage; literally, "to cross over."
Yane	Roof.
Yane-shita . . .	Roof-beams.
Yashiki	A lot of ground upon which a house stands. An enclosure for a Daimio's residence.

Yedo-gawara . .	.	Yedo tile.
Yen	.	A coin; equals one dollar.
Yen-gawa . . .	.	Verandah.
Yen-riyo . .	.	Reserve.
Yen-zashiki . .	.	End-parlor.
Yō-ba	.	Privy; literally, "place for business."
Yoshi	.	A kind of reed.
Yoshi-do . . .	.	A screen made of yoshi.
Yu-dono . . .	.	Bath-room.
Yuka-shita . .	.	The beams supporting the first floor.

図解300
明治・日本人の住まいと暮らし
モースが魅せられた美しく豊かな住文化
JAPANESE HOMES AND THEIR SURROUNDINGS
with ILLUSTRATIONS by EDWARD S. MORSE

2017年5月31日　初版第1刷発行

企画	大槻武志［阿吽社中］
編集	阿吽社
	602-0017 京都市上京区衣棚通上御霊前下ル上木ノ下町73-9
	電話 075-414-8951　FAX 075-414-8952
	URL: aunsha.co.jp　E-mail: info@aunsha.co.jp
発行者	勝丸裕哉
発行所	紫紅社
	605-0089 京都市東山区古門前通大和大路東入ル元町367
	電話 075-541-0206　FAX 075-541-0209
	URL: http://www.artbooks-shikosha.com/
DTP	トーヨー企画
印刷	モリモト印刷

Copyright © AUNSHA 2017, Printed in Japan
ISBN978-4-87940-625-5　C0039
定価はカバーに表示してあります
本書のコピー・スキャン・デジタル化等の無断複製を禁じます